A Guide to Barcelona's
Passeig de Gràcia

A mile of culture, fashion and leisure

With the collaboration of:

A Guide to Barcelona's Passeig de Gràcia
1st edition, 2014

Original edition in Catalan:
Guia del passeig de Gràcia de Barcelona

© 2014, ICG Marge, SL
© ICG Marge, SL / Ajuntament de Barcelona

Ajuntament de Barcelona
Editorial and Publishing Council of the city of Barcelona: Jaume Ciurana i Llevadot, Jordi Martí i Galbis, Marc Puig i Guàrdia, Albert Ortas i Serrano, Miquel Guiot i Rocamora, Jordi Joly i Lena, Vicente Guallart i Furió, Àngel Miret i Serra, Marta Clari i Padrós, Josep Lluís Alay i Rodríguez, José Pérez Freijo, Pilar Roca i Viola
Communication and Citizen Service Director: Marc Puig
Imaging and Editorial Services Director: José Pérez Freijo

Direcció d'Imatge i Serveis Editorials de l'Ajuntament de Barcelona
Passeig de la Zona Franca, 66 - 08038 Barcelona
Tel. +34-934 023 131 - www.bcn.cat/barcelonallibres
ISBN: 978-84-9850-638-9

Marge Books
Publishing director: David Soler
Managing editors: Hèctor Soler, Neus Piñol
Translator: Berni Armstrong
Make-up editor: Mercedes Lara
Printed by: Impremta Pagès (Anglès, Girona)

València, 558, àtic 2a - 08026 Barcelona
Tel. +34-932 449 130 - margebooks.com

ISBN: 978-84-15340-94-2
D.L.: B-26837-2014

Contents

Prologue

Barcelona has always been recognised as a city that is modern, dynamic, open to the world, entrepreneurial and highly commercial. I am sure you will realise, as you leaf through this guide, that Passeig de Gràcia is one of the best examples of all that.

Passeig de Gràcia is much more than a street. It is a quality commercial hub, where you will find some of the city's most iconic buildings. An avenue that symbolises Barcelona and which is admired by all who visit the city.

It is one of the best examples, in my opinion, of that harmonious combination of culture, architecture, tradition, commerce and individuality which is so characteristic of us. A true meeting-point thoroughfare packed with world-benchmark establishments that lies alongside a wide range of artistic and culinary offers and where creative and innovative events such as *Shopping Night* are organised.

It is along these lines that I would like to take the opportunity to express my gratitude to the Friends of Passeig de Gràcia Association, for all their effort and commitment, and to all the individuals, businesses and organisations, for their daily work to ensure the avenue continues to be one of Barcelona's true commercial, tourist, cultural and social driving forces.

Xavier Trias
The Mayor of Barcelona

Presentation

With its mile of shops, emblematic buildings, fine restaurants and Mediterranean lifestyle, the *Passeig de Gràcia* is one of the most renowned and important commercial and cultural centres in the world. Its national and international reputation has contributed to making Barcelona one of the most esteemed cities.

The singularity of *Passeig de Gràcia* is largely due to its location on the *Eixample*, the area that formed the backbone of Barcelona's early urban development, along with the modernist architecture of its first buildings and its role as a meeting place for the social life of many of Barcelona's inhabitants. Through its wide range of social, commercial and cultural activities, over more than a hundred and eighty years, *Passeig de Gràcia* has become an important showcase for Barcelona. It is an avenue where you can find the elegance of history at every step of the way.

It is a reference point for the people of Barcelona, it brings together in one place many important national and international companies and it forms part of an unmissable tourist route for visitors to the city.

We are sure that this guide will be a useful and practical tool for exploring the *Passeig de Gràcia* whatever aspect of it interests you, whether you are here for culture (visiting its buildings and museums) for the glamour of its commercial establishments, or for a taste of its exquisite restaurants. Above all, this is a guide which invites you to stroll along the avenue and allows you to identify each of the components you will meet along the way, elements that make up the heart of cosmopolitan Barcelona.

Lluís Sans
Friends of Passeig de Gràcia
President
www.barcelonapasseigdegracia.com

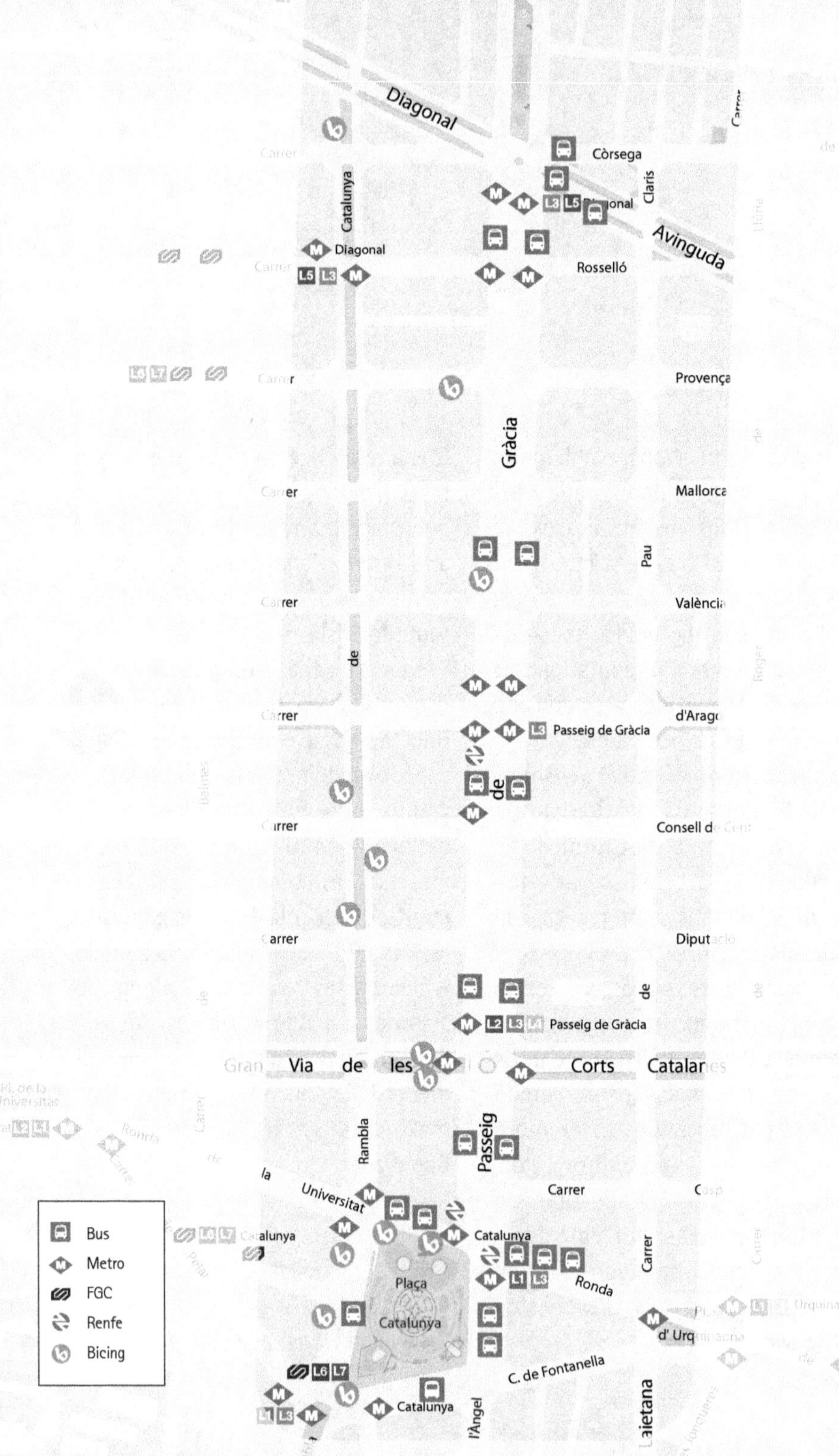

Diagonal
Carrer
Catalunya
Còrsega
Claris
Avinguda
M
M
L3 L5 Diagonal
M Diagonal
L5 L3 M
Rosselló
M M
Provença
Gràcia
Mallorca
Pau
València
de
d'Aragó
M M
M M L3 Passeig de Gràcia
de
Consell de Cent
Diputació
de
M L2 L3 L4 Passeig de Gràcia
Gran Via de les Corts Catalanes
M M
Pl. de la Universitat
Universitat L2 L1
Ronda
de
Rambla
Passeig
Carrer
Cosp
Universitat
M
M
Catalunya
Catalunya
M L1 L3 Ronda
Pl. Urquinaona
M L1 Urquinaona
M d'Urquinaona
Plaça
Catalunya
C. de Fontanella
Laietana
L6 L7
M
L1 L3 M
M Catalunya
l'Angel
Bus
M Metro
FGC
Renfe
Bicing
L6 L7 Catalunya

The Passeig de Gràcia
History, elegance and modernity

Towards the end of the 19th Century, two people might take twenty-five minutes to walk the section of *Passeig de Gràcia* from the *Gran Via* to *Carrer Diputació*. This was not because of the crowds of people impeding their progress, but rather because of the number of times they would have to stop to greet friends and acquaintances. Because if there's one thing that *Passeig de Gràcia* has always had, it is "status"; it is *the* place to be.

From 1860, when the old city walls were demolished, Barcelona did not stop growing and, in the process, absorbing the towns and villages surrounding it. *Passeig de Gràcia* was created from the need for better communications between the old village of *Gràcia* and the city centre. A major urban artery, it swiftly became one of the most important leisure and commercial areas in the city. It ran from the *Hotel Colón* on *Plaça Catalunya*, past the *Jardín de las Delicias*, the

[1] Francesc Pujols i Morgades (1882–1962), Catalan writer and philosopher.

Camps Elisis, the *Teatre Tívoli*, the *Teatre Novetats*, the *Jardí d'Euterpe* and the buildings of the "*Mansana de la Discòrdia*" until it reached *Palau Robert* at the very top of the street. The bourgeoisie of Barcelona, enriched largely thanks to capital arriving from the South American colonies, started a refined aesthetic competition aimed at recovering the lost splendour of the city by commissioning houses from leading modernist architects, among which the most notable was that architectural genius of the 20th Century, Antoni Gaudí, who designed the *Casa Milà*, popularly known as *La Pedrera*. All of these buildings converted the *Passeig de Gràcia* into a veritable open-air work of art.

However, *Passeig de Gràcia* and its surroundings have always had two other great vocations: a commitment to commerce and culture. Witness to the latter being the numerous first-class museums and exhibition spaces in the area such as the *Fundació Tàpies*, the *Museu Egipci* or the *Fundació Suñol*. The most prestigious commercial enterprises in Barcelona set up premises on the avenue from its very beginnings. Some, like *Santa Eulalia*, are still there, thriving alongside prestigious international brands such as Valentino or Chanel (who are well aware of the great cachet offered by having a branch along the *Passeig de Gràcia*). Barcelona having become one of the great world tourist attractions has led to a proliferation of hotels and luxury apartments in the area offering accommodation in this historic and artistic area, where, in a single boulevard, the city offers luxury and glamour, leisure and culture, tradition and modernity.

A brief history of *Passeig de Gràcia*

Passeig de Gràcia follows an ancient Roman road that united *Barcino* (as Barcelona was known then) with *Sant Cugat.* In the Middle Ages this road became known as the *Path of Jesus*, because it led to the Franciscan convent of *Santa Maria de Jesús*, which was located on the block that today runs from the streets known as *Consell de Cent* to *Aragó.* After that, it became the *Path to Gràcia*, continuing uphill until it reached the village of that name. The first urbanised section of *Passeig de Gràcia* was inaugurated in 1827. It was 1,550 metres long and 42 wide, divided into five lanes by six rows of trees planted with military precision. The central area was reserved for pedestrians and two lanes on either side were for carriages. Slowly, gardens and other leisure installations sprang up along it. Early on Sundays, the people of Barcelona would gather there, en masse, to

The *Passeig de Gràcia* in 1874

stroll along the boulevard and take a drink from one of the frequent water fountains. In 1860, Queen Isabel II laid the foundation stone for the city's expansion project, known as the *Eixample*, designed by Ildefons Cerdà, and the first houses and palaces were built along the avenue. The streets along the *Eixample* had an unprecedented width (at least 20 m for each street) and chamfered corners, a novelty in the history of urbanism. The proliferation of ground floor commercial pre-

The *Passeig de Gràcia* in 1915

Passeig de Gràcia around 1930

View of Passeig de Gràcia from Plaça de Catalunya around 1930

dernist buildings such as *La Pedrera*, as well as the arrival of its emblematic art deco streetlamps combined with public benches. Contemporary reaction was very mixed. Well into the 20th Century, there were eulogies as well as harsh criticism of the extravagance of some buildings. Throughout the rest of that century, major reforms were carried out along the avenue which resulted in the disappearance of the trams that had travelled along it and the broadening of the lateral pedestrian walkways allowing more people to stroll along one of the most famous and profitable avenues in the world.

mises happened towards the end of the century. That was also the period that saw an explosion of singular mo-

The cradle of modernism

The great industrial development of Catalonia in the 19th Century, coupled with a huge increase of population due to waves of immigration sparked by work linked to the Universal Exposition of Barcelona in 1888, along with the prosperity of many businesses and the early days of a political movement defending Catalan national interests were all catalysts that inspired a series of artists (sculptors and architects, but also poets, musicians and painters) who were open to new European artistic currents to demonstrate their personal talent and creativity with total freedom. Urbanising the *Passeig de Gràcia* became a motive for pri-

Casa Amatller, in 1900. Dining room with Antoni and Teresa Amatller

Casa Comalat

Ceramic works in Casa Lleó Morera

Detail from the ceramics in Casa Lleó Morera

de and showing off among the new bourgeoisie, enriched thanks to the Americas or the power of industries such as textiles. They did not hesitate in financing the most daring projects. Catalan *modernisme* (a style which in other European countries was known as the modern style, *jugendstil* or *art nouveau)*, with its taste for sinuous shapes inspired by nature, filled this avenue with buildings having chimneys, roofs and fortified towers with the appearance of warriors or sleeping dragons; all of which give *Passeig de Gràcia* its unique character. Modernism not only expressed itself in the façades, but also in the interior of the buildings, in the finishes, mosaics, decoration, furniture, accessories or sculptures. Competition between patrons and top-level architects (Domènech i Montaner, Puig i Cadafalch, Enric Sagnier or Antoni Gaudí, among others) reached its apogee in the "Mansana de la Discòrdia", between *Carrer Consell de Cent* and *Carrer Aragó*. The daring of architects designing such buildings as the *Casa Lleó Morera*, the *Casa Amatller* or the *Casa Batlló* gave rise to three jewels that no modern visitor to *Passeig de Gràcia* could fail to admire.

La Pedrera around 1930

A commercial and gastronomic avenue

Over recent decades, *Passeig de Gràcia* has joined a select list of the most important commercial streets in the world: the *Via Condotti* in Rome; the *Via Montenapoleone* in Milan; the *Champs Elysées* in Paris; New Bond Street in London; Fifth Avenue in New York and *Passeig de Gràcia* in Barcelona. Along this avenue can be found high class apartments and the best hotels such as the *Casa Fuster*, the *Majestic & Spa* or the *Mandarin Oriental*. There are also leading luxury clothes and accessories firms from Gucci to Louis Vuitton, through Yves Saint Laurent to Carolina Herrera, Loewe or Valentino; jewellers such as Tiffany, Cartier o Bulgari, or perfumers such as Chanel. All share the avenue with leading names in mass consumerism like

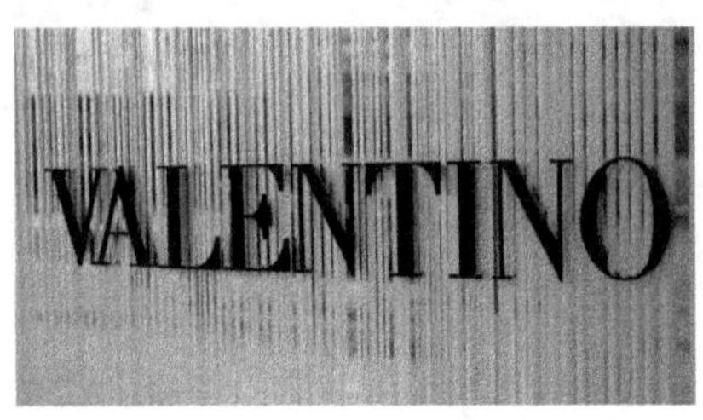

Zara, in the fashion world, or Apple, the technology giant. They all compete to place their flagship stores in the best and most strategic places along the avenue. However, the *Passeig de Gràcia* is also home to the offices of professionals as well as to corporate national and international headquarters from all the industrial and service sectors.

This commercial world is complemented by a varied gastronomic offering in which we can find everything from establishments with Michelin stars, such as *Moments* or *Roca Moo*, to more traditional Catalan and Mediterranean cuisine, along with tapas bars. Its location among hundred-year-

The Mandarin Oriental

old palaces and the splendour of neo-classicist and modernist gems makes *Passeig de Gràcia* one of the economic centres of the city and a must visit attraction for anyone seeking a cocktail of luxury and commercial vitality combined with tradition.

Culture and new trends

The classicist and avant-garde nature of *Passeig de Gràcia* and, above all, its cosmopolitan character make it the ideal setting for very different celebrations and events.

The Fira del Llibre (second-hand book fair). Started in 1952, this fair, organised by the Catalan Guild of Antique Book Sellers, is the longest established of the celebrations held on the avenue. For a fortnight, in the month of October, booksellers set up stands to offer the public their treasures: second-hand books, difficult to find titles, out of print volumes and authentic

collectors' pieces all tempt book lovers, year after year, despite the unstoppable advance of new technologies.

Setmana del Barret (hat week). This is an initiative started by the classic fabric and fashion shop *Gra-*

tacós. For a week in April, they invite designers to work inside their shop so the public can appreciate the latest designs in hats and headgear. The event is aimed at publicising the artistic side of the millinery profession.

Verema (wine harvest). Similar to the *Vendanges Montaigne* in Paris or the *Vendemmia* in Milan, the *Friends of Passeig de Gràcia Association* has organised this event every September from 2011. The event is restricted exclusively to clients invited by the shops participating in the celebration, which consists of bringing together luxury products and the finest still and sparkling wines in the world.

The Shopping Night. One night a year, shops along the whole avenue open their doors allowing customers to enjoy shopping in a unique atmosphere. From eight o'clock in the evening until one o'clock in the morning, it becomes possible to experience the nocturnal face of fashion combined with artistic and cultural activities such as painting, theatre or opera. The event was first held in 2010 and has not stopped growing since.

Museums and singular collections

Passeig de Gràcia (and its surrounding area) houses exhibition spaces and little arty nooks that are a must for all lovers of art and culture, as well as just the plain curious. The **Museu de la Perruqueria** (hairdressing) and the **Museu del Perfum** both have on display bottles, flasks,

Museu de la Perruqueria

Palau Robert

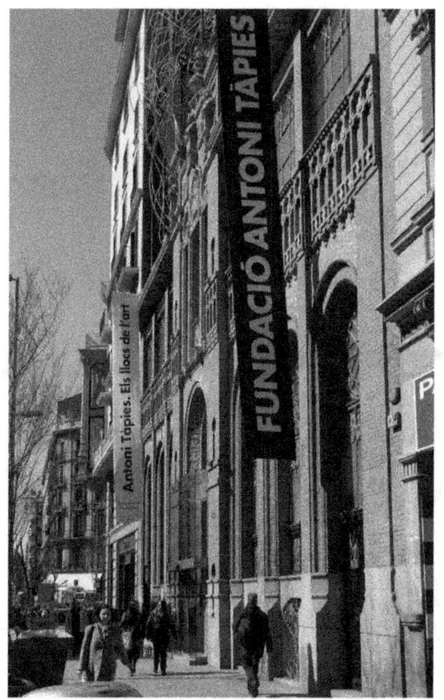

recipients and articles that offer visitors a voyage from prehistory right up to the latest technical innovations and the most famous brands of today. Two great internationally renowned Catalan artists give their names to two very different foundations. The **Fundació Tàpies** houses the permanent collection of the *informaliste* painter Antoni Tàpies, as well as offering temporary exhibitions and having an excellent art library. The **Fundació Frederic Mompou**, located in the flat where this musician and composer lived, is aimed at fa-

miliarising young musicians with his work. The **Fundació Suñol** offers exhibitions from different disciplines of national and international contemporary art.

At the **Museu Egipci**, more than a thousand items offer visitors the possibility to be transported back to the civilisation of the Pharaohs. The **Fundació Institut Amatller d'Art Hispànic** and the **La Pedrera** cultural centre hold important exhibitions, lecture cycles, poetry recitals, music concerts and audiovisual projections; while at the **Palau Robert** can be found permanent and temporary exhibitions in its more than 1,000 m^2, divided into four exhibition spaces, as well as a tourist office which can inform you about any topic related to the *Passeig de Gràcia*, Barcelona or Catalonia.

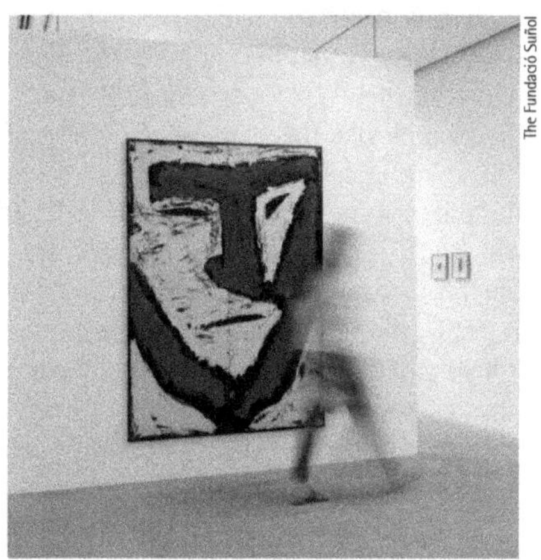
The Fundació Suñol

Metro: L1 (Catalunya), L2 (Passeig de Gràcia), L3 (Catalunya, Passeig de Gràcia), L4 (Passeig de Gràcia), L5 (Diagonal)
www.tmb.cat

Bus: 6, 7, 15, 16, 17, 20, 22, 24, 28, 33, 34, 39, 43, 44, 45, 47, 63, 67, 68, 544, V17, H10, H12, N4, N5, Bus Turístic: north and south routes
www.tmb.cat
www.barcelonabusturistic.cat

Renfe (railway): Plaça Catalunya, Passeig de Gràcia
www.renfe.com

FGC (railway): Catalunya, Provença-La Pedrera
www.fgc.cat

Taxis: 931131920 / 933033033 / 933222222

From Barcelona Airport to Passeig de Gràcia:
Aerobús: www.aerobusbcn.com
Railway: Line R2 North Airport (Rodalies Renfe), www.renfe.com

From Port Vell to passeig de Gràcia: L3 (Drassanes) y L4 (Barceloneta)

Bicing (bike hire): passeig de Gràcia 61 (València) / passeig de Gràcia 89 (Provença) / Plaça Catalunya, 10-11
www.bicing.cat

Car Parks:
Saba Gràcia I, Diagonal (Jardinets)
Saba Gràcia II, Gran Via-Aragó
Saba Gràcia III, Aragó-Rosselló
www.saba.cat

Sea & mountain / Rivers Besòs & Llobregat

We are not talking here about a traditional dish, or a *paella* combining meat and fish. This is the way that the people of Barcelona indicate where a place or address is located geographically. This is particularly true of those in the centre of the city. Barcelona is limited in the North by **Tibidabo** , in the south by the **Mediterranean** , in the East by the River **Besòs,** and in the West by the River **Llobregat.** These are the inhabitant's compass points. So, any place located along the streets running perpendicular to *Passeig de Gràcia,* for example, will be referred to as mountain or sea depending whether it is on the North or South side. Just as any address on the *Passeig de Gràcia,* or parallel streets, will be referred to as being on the Besòs or Llobregat side, depending on whether it is on the East or West side.

Symbols

- Bank
- Cinema
- Shop
- Art Gallery
- Singular Building
- Pharmacy
- Hotel
- Tourist Information
- Museum/Monument
- Restaurant/Bar
- Theatre
- Others

From Plaça de Catalunya to Gran Via de les Corts Catalanes

Numbers 1-11

1

🏛 **Banco Español de Crédito building** (1942). Until 2003, this neoclassic building, the work of architect Eusebi Bona i Puig, was the head office of the Banco Español de Crédito (Banesto) in Barcelona.

Curious fact: The *Hotel Colon*, featured in Orwell's "Homage to Catalonia", once stood on this spot. Inaugurated in 1902, it was the place where the first radio broadcasting station in Spain, EAJ-1 Radio Barcelona, was set up. The building was demolished in 1940.

🛍 **Apple Store.** Since 2012, the iconic white apple with a bite out of it has stood at the entrance to this emblematic shop. With 2500 m² of space, this is the largest Apple Centre in the south of Europe. The ground floor is always full of people eager to try out the latest models of computers, tablets and mobile phones made by the company founded by Steve Jobs. The first floor is for repairs and the basement is for all kinds of accessories, such as bags and cases, etc.

Adidas Store. This is the official store in Barcelona of the well-known brand of sports clothing worn by such star players as Barcelona's Leo Messi.

Curious fact: This address was once home to the monumental *Café Alhambra* (1891), until 1906 when the Belio Gracia Brothers, Mariano and Manuel, transformed it into the headquarters of the cinematography company Belio-Graff. It was inaugurated with the projection of eight films made by *Pathé Frères*. It closed in 1912.

Banco Santander. This is the head office in Barcelona of the bank founded in the Cantabrian city whose name it bears. It is one of the most important banks in the Euro zone.

Casa Puig Colom (1913). Although it has gone through numerous changes over the years, including the addition of two further floors to the four it originally had, this building, designed by Josep Font i Gumà maintains a certain aristocratic air. From its beginnings until the mid-1950s, the ground floor was occupied by the incredibly popular baker's the *Forn de Sant Jaume*, one of the most renowned cake shops in the city.

Bershka. This boutique has a wide range of colourful and sporty clothes for youth as well as shoes and accessories for both sexes.

🛍 **H&M.** This Swedish-based boutique, with its combination of good design and excellent prices, specialises in clothes, cosmetics and everyday accessories. It also has stuff for kids.

🏛 **Generali building** (1950). This imposing building, with its 21 floors and 75 m tall tower, was originally designed to house *Banco Vitalicio*, along with a still extant shopping area (the *Galeria Condal*), a now forgotten performance space and offices and apartments. The work of architect Lluís Bonet i Garí, it is one of the most notable examples in the city of the architecture of the Franco period. The façades are covered in granite from Galicia and local stone from Montjuïc, along with several sculptural groups and statues which adorn the main elements. It was one of the first skyscrapers in the city and was its tallest building until the mid-1970s. In 2009, two insurance companies *Vitalicio* and *Estrellas* merged to become the *Sociedad Generali*.

Curious fact: In order to build this building, it was necessary to demolish the *Palau Samà*, belonging to the Marquis of Marianao. A marble fountain from the palace was conserved which you can see in café *La Nou*, within the *Galeria Condal*.

Galeria Condal. Passageways connect *Passeig de Gràcia* with the *Gran Via de les Corts Catalanes* and lead to the three staircases up to the building's offices. In the centre, is the cafe-restaurant *La Nou* where you can relax and have a coffee or lunch, far from the noise of the streets.

Stradivarius. Despite the name and logo evoking the world of music, Stradivarius is a reasonably priced clothes boutique for the young set.

McGregor. The characteristic tartan serves as a standard for this clothes shop for men, which, among other items, stocks tracksuits and polo necks.

Double Agent. A fashion boutique influenced by American styles. It offers clothes, shoes, bags, costume jewellery, cosmetics and accessories for young girls and adolescents in 200 m² of space distributed over three floors. This firm rejects the use of traditional publicity channels and has made its name largely through using social media to promote itself.

Piquadro. The very name is a synonym for Italian leather work. Wallets, handbags, travel bags, suitcases and accessories, for both men and women, all with an innovative and original design, are available in the more than a hundred boutiques the brand has in 50 countries.

Geox. This is one of the brands of shoes that have exploded onto the Spanish market in recent years. Originally from Italy, they have established themselves thanks to their innovative designs, especially their breathable soled sports shoes.
They have another shop at number 52.

Gran Via de les Corts Catalanes towards the Llobregat

Gran Via de les Corts Catalanes, 630

Farga. One of the longest standing cake shops and delicatessens in the city. In addition to the shop, it has a terrace and a restaurant which serves high-quality breakfast, lunch and dinners. There is another branch at the top of the *Passeig* on *Avinguda Diagonal* at number 391.

Gran Via de les Corts Catalanes, 605

Avenida Palace (1952) (4*). This classic hotel, with its spectacular golden lobby, was completely renovated in 2006. It has nine floors and 151 rooms, with all the usual services. Among the famous names who have stayed here were Ernest Hemingway, Joan Miró, Lizza Minnelli or The Beatles.

Monument to the Book. Work of the Catalan sculptor and poet Joan Brossa (1919-1998), this sculpture was created in 1994 as a commission from the second-hand book fair the *Fira del Llibre d'Ocasió Antic i Modern* which has been organised every autumn since 1952 by the booksellers guild the *Gremi de Llibreters de Vell de Catalunya*. A plaque with the signature of the latest writer invited to open the event is attached to the foot of the monument every year.

Observe and be seen: vanished cafes and theatres

Given the great popularity of the boulevard at the close of the 19th Century, there was a boom in the number of cafes and places to eat and drink, as well as numerous theatres there. Indeed, there were so many of the latter that one of the most popular dramatists of the time, Serafí Pitarra, said "there are now more theatres in the *Passeig* than people who go there". Today there only remains the *Tívoli*, the *Coliseum* and another, converted into a cinema, the *Comèdia*.

The leading theatre on the *Passeig* was the *Tívoli*, it later moved to *Carrer Casp*, where it remains today. In 1863, two other theatres were inaugurated: one, the *Teatre Prado Catalán*, set among gardens and with a capacity for an audience of 1,800. It had a circular stage, because it put on equestrian circuses. The other was the *Teatre Delicias*, in the *Criadero* gardens.

In 1869, the *Teatre Novedades* opened; it would become well renowned. Although it was originally on the corner with the *Ronda de Sant Pere*, in 1885 it was moved a street up to the corner with *Carrer Casp*, where it joined a cafè, a ballroom and a billiard hall. It could seat

an audience of 2,000 and, in addition to theatre, it held masked balls, concerts or political meetings. It was destroyed by bombing during the Spanish Civil War. It later reopened as a cinema and an amusement arcade, but finally closed in 2006.

In 1870, the *Teatro Español* was opened. Its entrance was in the passageway between numbers 26 and 24. Designed by the architect Antoni

Rovira i Trias, it was made of wood and could also hold 2,000 people. Its theatrical fare included drama, Italian opera or the Spanish light opera known as *Sarsuela*. In 1889, it was destroyed by fire.

The first cafè of all was the *Gran Café Hispano-Americano*, inaugurated in 1874, at number 38-40 (renamed the *Cafè Lisboa* in 1881). A little further down, on the corner with *Carrer Casp*, the *Gran Café Novedades* opened, spreading tables across the *Passeig*. It had room for twenty-three tables and, when it introduced a billiard hall, it became a spectacular success. The biggest, however, was the Alhambra Café, opened in 1891 at number 3 on the boulevard. One of the most important of these establishments was the *Cafè Torino*, located at number 18. Its owner was from Turin and it was he who introduced the custom of "having a vermouth" to Spain, a habit that was then typically Italian. The *Cafè Torino* had an awning and the sculptures on its façade, along with the interior decoration, were the work of Antoni Gaudí and Josep Puig i Cadafalch. In 1910, the Board of Barcelona Football Club chose the café as a place to celebrate their first Spanish championship. Between 1909 and 1960, the *Cafè Terminus*, decorated in a Neo-Arabic style, was the favourite meeting place for sports fans and intellectuals. The most famous cafe bar was that promoted by the modernist poet and painter Santiago Rusiñol, who lived at number 96, *La Puñalada* at nearby number 104, it closed down in 1998.

Cafè Torino

Bar La Puñalada

Gran Via de les Corts Catalanes, 595

The Coliseum (1923). Inaugurated as a cinema, it is still one of the largest in the city, although since 2006 it has generally been used as a theatre for large-scale shows or concerts. It was the first cinema in Spain to show a film with sound: *A Song of Paris* (1929), a Paramount film starring Maurice Chevalier. It is an example of the *monumentalist* architecture of the 1920s, the work of Catalan architect Francesc de Paula Bonet. It was inspired by the Paris Opera. Its great dome, flanked by two towers, is visible from a great distance as is its convex curving entrance. In front of the building, in the Gran Via de les Corts Catalanes Avenue, is the 10m high modern sculpture entitled *Encaix* (2003), a piece by artist Margarita Andreu. An inscription on the floor says: "To all the people killed in Fascist bombing raids on Barcelona (1937 - 1939) in the Civil War and to all victims of other wars".

Diputació

From Gran Via de les Corts Catalanes to Diputació

Numbers 13–19 bis

Gran Via

13

🏛 **Marcet Palace** (1890) / 🎞 **Cinema Comèdia.** This small palace, one of the few remaining examples of urban palace architecture on the *Eixample*, was designed by the architect Tiberi Sabater, in 1887, as a private home. After a complete overhaul in 1941 that only kept the original façade, it opened as the *Teatre Comedia* and in 1960 became the *Cinema Comedia*, which was split into three projection areas in 1983 and later, in 1995, into the current five. Eclectic in style, with classical and neo-plateresque elements, its main façade is on the chamfered corner of the *Gran Via* and *Passeig de Gràcia*. Note the convex coverings on the roofs of the corners and the ridges on the temple-like crest. The original structure had sumptuous gardens at the back which vanished when the adjacent buildings were built.

Curious fact: In front of the entrance to the cinema is one of the only two remaining Wallace Fountains in Barcelona (the other is on the *La Rambla de Santa Mònica*). These drinking

Central Fountain. The construction of this fountain, at the crossroads of *Passeig de Gràcia* and the *Gran Via*, formed part of the urban transformation brought about by the celebration, in the city, of the International Eucharistic Congress in 1952. The circular ornamental fountain, 13.5 metres in diameter, was overhauled in 2012 to increase the intensity of its lights and colours and optimise its consumption of energy.

fountains were part of a dozen that the philanthropist Sir Richard Wallace donated to the city when it hosted the Universal Exposition of 1888.

Lottusse. A brand of shoes originally from Mallorca. The company was founded in 1877 by Antoni Fluxà Figuerola. Over the years, in addition to its classic and elegant footwear, it has broadened its catalogue of products to include bags and accessories for women available through a network of boutiques on three continents.

Guess. This is an American company founded in Los Angeles in 1981 by the Marciano Brothers. It offers a youthful, sensual and adventurous style with a complete line of clothes and accessories for men, women and children. It also sells lingerie, perfumes and gifts. They have another shop at number 63.

Caramelo. Founded in 1969 with the aim of producing quality

rainproof clothing, it has become an international brand and has integrated collections for women by the Spanish designer Antonio Pernas.

La Baguetina Catalana. This takeaway food outlet specialises above all in sandwiches and slices of pizza; all at reasonable prices.

Tommy Hilfiger. A flagship boutique in Barcelona for this US brand which began by making jeans, but today offers clothes for the whole family in an informal and sporty style.

Banco Popular. The head office in Barcelona of this bank, created in 1926 in the capital of Spain, now headed by Ángel Ron and geared towards the retail banking

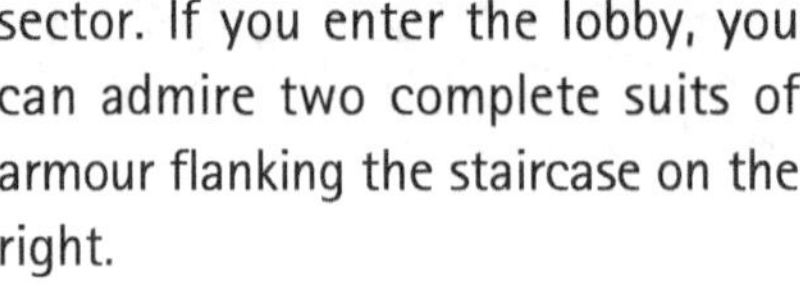

sector. If you enter the lobby, you can admire two complete suits of armour flanking the staircase on the right.

🏛 **Barcelona Stock Exchange.** This granite and glass building is the head office of the Barcelona stock exchange, which functions as a secondary market to the Madrid stock exchange.

🛍 **Diesel.** Since its foundation, in 1987, it has been primarily famous for its jeans. However, it has become one of the most emblematic brands for many young people who also come here to buy underwear, accessories and shoes.

Carrer Diputació towards the River Llobregat

Diputació, 256
🛍 **Les Golfes.** This is the ideal place to buy handmade traditional dolls of all sizes and types.

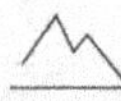

Diputació, 257
🏨 **Cristal Palace** (4*). This hotel has every convenience for travellers whether they are sightseers or here on business. It has a striking façade covered in glass panels.

From Diputació
to Consell de Cent

Numbers 21–33

21

 *La Unión y el Fénix* **building** (1931). French in influence, with a 19th Century affinity, the building was designed as the head offices of the insurance companies the *Unión* and the *Fénix*. It was the work of the architect Eusebi Bona i Puig. It is the only semicircular chamfered corner on the boulevard and is crowned by a very characteristic dome. Its ornamental elements are of classical inspiration: the phoenix on top of the dome, the double columns with Corinthian capitals and the sculptural groups on the fourth floor, by Frederic Marès, representing life, industry, agriculture, the arts, navigation and death.

 Brandy Melville. This Italian fashion boutique for young people was inaugurated, provisionally, in 2013 as a pop-up store, but it was so successful that it became permanent.

 Tumi. Founded, in 1975, as a brand selling travel accessories (suitcases, handbags or wallets), this US firm has constantly expanded its catalogue, which now includes articles for writing.

 La Vaca Paca. This is a well-established restaurant with an exterior terrace that offers an open buffet at very reasonable prices.

 Femina building. The ground floor of this building was inaugurated in 1929 as the *Femina* cinema, with an access also on *Carrer Diputació* at number 259. It was overhauled by the architect Antoni de Moragas in 1948 and destroyed by fire in 1991. It was rebuilt in 1999, to a design by architects Carlos Ferrater and Joan Guibernau, who created new functional and expressive apartments, with transition spaces between the ancient and modern.

 Max Mara / Marina Rinaldi. "Style isn't a cut, it's an attitude!" With this statement, the Italian fashion designer Marina Rinaldi gained the heart of many women whose shapes do not seem to be catered for by the majority of fashion brands for women. This interconnected double-shop has, on one side, *prêt-à-porter* fashion for the well-off contemporary urban woman and on the other side it offers its larger sizes. They also sell bags and accessories.

 Casa Malagrida (1908). A splendid example of a modernist house designed for multi-family occupancy. It was the work of architect Joaquim Codina Matalí, commissioned by the tobacco baron from the Pre-Pyrenean town of Olot, Manuel Malagrida, who made his fortune in Argentina with the cigarette factory *Centenario*. The decoration of the house combines a Pyrenean eagle with an Andean Condor as well as anthropomorphic representations of Spain and Argentina, the crown and the Phrygian cap respectively. The main floor is notable for its sumptuous façade, with balus-

trades and galleries richly decorated with floral motifs. At the top there is a dome reminiscent of a mansard.

🛍 **COS.** This is the high-end brand of H&M. With a surface area of some 600 m². Here, the classics are reinvented and the latest trends in clothes and accessories for men, women and children are sold. Cos has a very particular style, reflecting the Scandinavian roots of the brand. The palette of colours is measured and the manufacture of each garment is meticulous, adding a touch of contemporary elegance.

🛍 **Twin-Set Simona Barbieri.** An Italian boutique offering their range of clothes, lingerie, swimwear and accessories for feminine, sophisticated and romantic women.

🛍 **Nike.** The official shop in Barcelona of one of the most important sports clothes companies in the world. Among the stars who wear their gear is the tennis player Rafa Nadal. Here can be found all kinds of trainers, sports clothes and accessories.

🏢 **Bcn Design** (5*). In order to turn the building into a hotel, it had to be completely restructured by the architecture and interior design studio of Xavier Claramunt, who transformed it into this small elegant and modern hotel-boutique with 65 guest rooms.

🛍 **H.E. by Mango.** One of the four Mango boutiques on *Passeig de Gràcia*, this one specialises in clothes for men. It has some 800 m² between the ground floor and basement.
H.E., in Latin, stood for *homini emerito.* If you believe you are a man who deserves esteem, this is your store.

🏛 *Union des Assurances de Paris* **building** (1913). It is worth a careful look at this building, the work of the modernist architect Enric Sagnier i Villavecchia, both for its

singularity and, above all, for its upper floors which were added when the former *Ladies in Black* convent school was transformed into the head offices in Barcelona of the Paris-based Union insurance company. Two vertical bodies, finished in stone reliefs, frame the top two floors; one with windows culminating in arches and ceramic decorations and the other with an open gallery supported by columns with stucco finishes. The ground floor was also modified using the same criteria. Openings in the two angles of the previously solid chamfered corner were added with elegant twin columns in pink marble.

¶ Brown 33.

An Italian restaurant spread across three floors complements a terrace where, in addition to pizzas, pastas and other typically Italian and Mediterranean dishes, you can also try some fine hamburgers.

Equity Point Centric Hostel.

This is a youth hostel with all kinds of accommodation from single, double and shared rooms for 4, 6 or 8 travellers.

Kiehl's.

This is a cosmetics shop decorated in the purest New York style (the chain was founded there in 1851). It has neon-lit letters and even a mural painting of the Statue of Liberty. Available here are facial, corporal and capillary treatments, special products for babies, sportsmen and women, sun creams and the famous Musk Fragrance.

Bench-lampposts

The well-known bench-lampposts along the *Passeig de Gràcia* are often attributed to Gaudí. However, despite the mosaics on the benches, the modernist shapes and their location, there is no truth in this. The bench-lampposts along the boulevard, together with those you can find in other parts of Barcelona *(Avinguda Gaudí* and *Passeig Lluís Companys),* were, in fact, designed in 1906 by the architect Pere Falqués i Urpí (1850-1916). There are thirty-two of these sculptural elements in wrought iron. Their decoration includes the city's coat of arms, along with the characteristic spiralling *coup de fouet* representing floral motifs.

Of great importance in the early 20th Century, during the development of the *Passeig de Gràcia,* these lamps have been losing prominence over the years, mainly due to reforms in the 1970s. Now, despite being a symbol of the centre of the city, they survive, as best they can, the damage caused by the huge volume of traffic, both vehicular and pedestrian, in the area. During the above-mentioned reform, other benches, inspired by Pere Falqués' originals and made using white mosaics with plant pots, but without lampposts, were placed on some of the corners of the boulevard.

Carrer Consell de Cent towards the River Llobregat

≋

Consell de Cent, 308

🛍 **Torrons Vicens.** This is the ideal shop in which to taste a very traditional Spanish sweet: the *torró*, a kind of nougat. Making their products by hand since 1775, the Vicens company, originally from a small town in the interior of Catalonia called Agramunt, offer *torrons* for every taste: coconut, chocolate, yoghurt, custard or marzipan, among others.

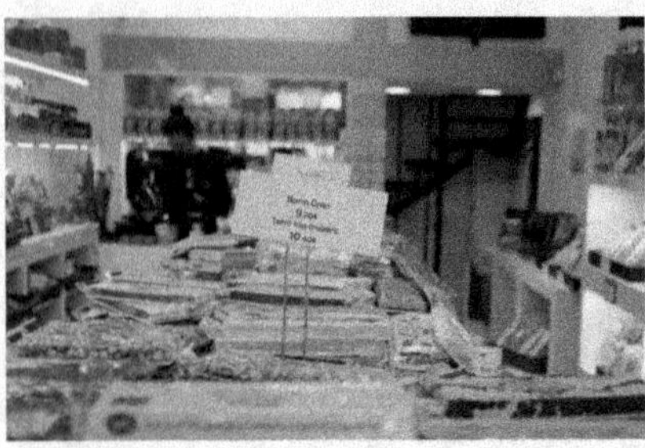

🍴 **La cuina d'en Garriga.** This exquisite delicatessen with its cheeses, dairy products, wines, foie gras, charcuterie, fruit, vegetables and kitchen utensils was the idea of Helena Garriga, who wanted to recreate the atmosphere of her family kitchen. As a symbol for her company she chose the soda siphon, a very popular item in the 1920s and 30s. Note that in the interior there is small, very chic restaurant with only a few tables.

🛍 **Majoral.** The jeweller Enric Majoral began making jewellery on the island of *Formentera* (Balearic Islands) in the 1970s, inspired by the energy and light of the Mediterranean and his great creativity. Today, his son Roc Majoral, continues to innovate and make pieces that echo natural elements such as seaweeds, sea urchins or fishing boats.

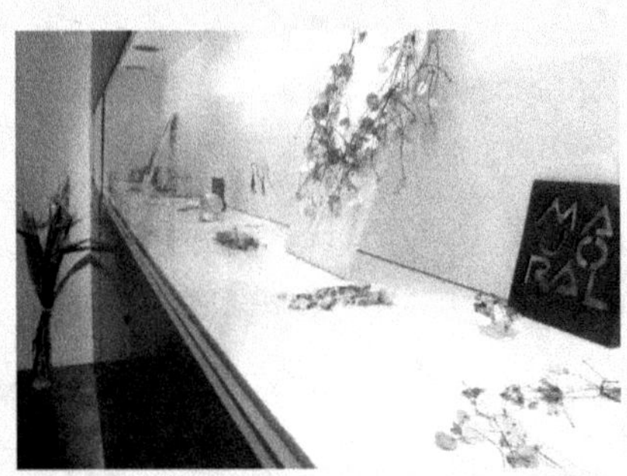

⛰

Consell de Cent, 347

🖼 **Galeria Jordi Barnadas.** An art gallery inaugurated in 1992 that specialises in contemporary, preferably figurative, artists.

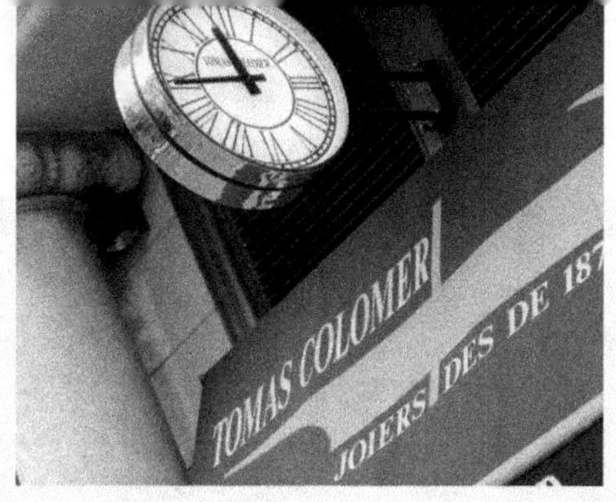

The work of some forty artists is on permanent display in the exhibition hall on the ground floor, where you will find oil and acrylic paintings on canvas or wood by aspiring or recognised artists.

Monday morning and Sundays closed.

Consell de Cent, 349

Sala Dalmau. Although it has maintained the name, the current gallery has no connection with the historic *Galeries Dalmau* (1911-1930), which brought the first Cubist exhibitions to Barcelona, welcomed foreign artists from Paris (residents or merely passing through) during the First World War and which exported to the world the work of Catalan artists such as Joan Miró. Today the gallery, opened in 1979, is oriented towards recovering artists of the historical avant-garde, while also dedicating itself to contemporary artistic figures.

Tomás Colomer. This name is on the face of an eye-catching clock that sticks out from the façade to draw attention to this jeweller's, founded in 1870, it is run today by the fifth generation of the Colomer family. Classic high-class watches and jewels.

Consell de Cent, 351

Aristocrazy. This is the youth brand of Suárez the jeweller's. Originally from Bilbao they set up in Madrid in 1982 and specialise in jewellery and deluxe watches. Since 2010, Aristocrazy has appealed to a public with a limited budget and more extreme tastes. It occupies some 200 m^2 of the shop, which conserves some of the original elements of this former pharmacy.

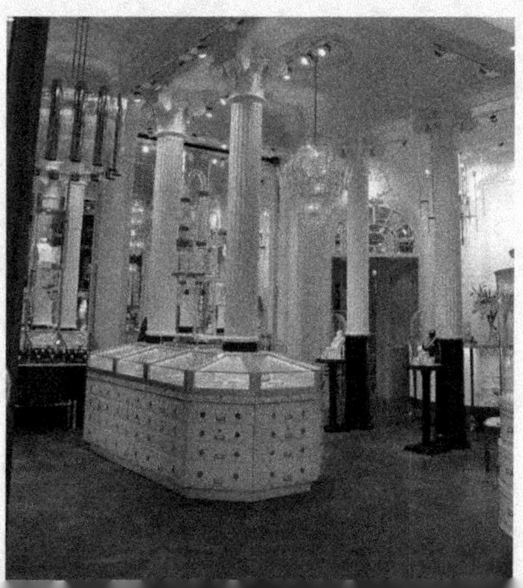

The "Mansana de la Discòrdia"

"The Mansana de la Discòrdia gave our most important architects the opportunity to excel themselves deliriously."

The industrialist Rafael Puget to the writer Josep Pla in *Un senyor de Barcelona* (1945)

Casa Lleó Morera, 1905–1910

At the beginning of the 20th Century, the section of the *Passeig de Gràcia* between *Consell de Cent* and *Aragó* received the popular name *La Mansana de la Discòrdia* reflecting the Greek "apple of discord" myth while punning on the Spanish word for a city block. The same pun gave NYC its nickname of the Big Apple. The people of Barcelona were astonished to see how, one after another, three of the best architects of the time had transformed, in an extraordinary way, the façades of three buildings belonging to leading members of the bourgeoisie. First there was Josep Puig i Cadafalch who, in 1901, was commissioned by the chocolate manufacturer, Antoni Amatller

i Costa, to transform number 41. The result was the **Casa Amatller**, with its highly provocative and characteristic step-shaped gable, which could equally be seen as an echo of formal influences from the low countries or of a candy bar with some of the squares of chocolate broken off. Four years later, in 1905, it was Lluís Domènech i Montaner who designed a splendid **Casa Lleó Morera** at number 35, on the corner of *Consell de Cent*. To crown the building there is a spectacular *tempietto* (a small temple like structure). The façade was filled with reliefs showing feminine figures, among which, the most notable, at street level, were two semi-clad women holding large vases; the source of many ribald comments. A university porter asked to take a package to that address was said to have asked the professor: "Isn't that the place with the two women with huge jugs of holy water?" The statues disappeared during the Franco period.

Casa Amatller, 1900

The third house in this block of contention was the **Casa Batlló,** designed by Antoni Gaudí i Cornet. Right next door to the *Casa Amatller,* the textile factory owner Josep Batlló gave carte blanche to the then young architect to use all his imagination and creativity in creating a façade full of organic and mysterious elements that is also open to numerous interpretations. Was it a representation of Carnival, with its masks and confetti? The most widely recognised interpretation reads the building as symbolising the fight between St George (the patron saint of Catalonia) and the dragon. The coloured ceramic roof being interpreted as the dragon's back. The balconies and columns represent the bones the dragon was guarding in his cave and the tower with its cross symbolises the Knight's lance. "I have visited the *Casa Batlló* and it still seems like a dream to me. In its interior, all the lines are curved. There are ceilings which resemble great vents. There are innumerable shapes inspired by mushrooms", says the protagonist of the book *A Gentleman of Barcelona* by the writer Josep Pla, astounded by the architectural and decorative boldness of Antoni Gaudí's genius. These three buildings must be one of the sections of street with the greatest concentration of talent and originality in the world. However, the contrast of styles between these buildings generated much popular controversy which filled the satirical columns in the newspapers of the early 20th Century.

From Consell de Cent to Aragó

Numbers 35–45

🏛 🏛 **Casa Lleó Morera** (1906). Nicknamed a *"Palau de la Música* in miniature", this house is one of the finest modernist gems in the city. The work of Lluís Domènech i Montaner, the architect who designed the con-cert hall from which it received its nickname, the building is particularly notable for the temple-like structure on its roof. This exceeded the height permitted by Barcelona City Hall and needed special permission. Also of note is the copious decoration on the

façade which includes various representations of the mulberry leaf (in al-
lusion to the family name - *morera* is
Catalan for mulberry) along with the
figures of small dragons. However, its
interior is even more impressive with
its stained glass, mosaics, ceramics,
sculptures, woodwork, marble, sgraf-
fitti, etc. created by artists and artisans
such as the sculptor Eusebi Arnau, the
mosaic artist Mario Maragliano or the
cabinetmaker Gaspar Homar, these
different applied arts illuminate the
building. Since 2014, the first floor
of the building has been open to the
public. There are four opportunities to

see it per day, but only for twenty-five
people at a time, so booking in advance is highly recommended.

Curious fact: The project was commissioned in 1902 by Francesca
Morera as a restructuring of the old
Casa Rocamora, which dated from
1864. On her death in 1904, her
son Albert Lleó i Morera continued
the work and it was he who finally
named the building. It was the only
one of the buildings on the *Mansana
de la Discòrdia* to win an architectural prize from Barcelona City Council.

 Loewe. This classic brand from
Madrid was founded in 1846. Ever
since, it has been offering its renowned leather bags, handkerchiefs,

wallets, *prêt-à-porter* clothes and other accessories associated with elegance and tradition.

 **Casa Mulleras** (1906). Very much more sober and classical than the buildings surrounding it, this house, designed by Enric Sagnier i Villavecchia, was also the result of a commission to renovate an older building, the *Casa Ramon Comas* (1868), which had been acquired by Ramon Mulleras, who wished to modernise it. The most prominent feature is a bay window on the main floor, which serves as a balcony for the first floor. On top, there is another balcony which allows you to walk around the exterior of the house.

Tenorio. A *brasserie* that defines itself as practising "Mediterranean and combined cuisines". It offers the advantage of its privileged location and its glorious terrace.

○ **Friends of Passeig de Gràcia.** Founded in 1952, is one of the oldest commercial associations in the city. From their headquarters on the second floor of this building,

they promote and defend the interests of their members and keep an eye on the state of the boulevard.

39

 **Casa Josefina Bonet** (1915). This building was built in 1887, but its façade was renovated in 1915 by the architect Marcel·lí Coquillat i Llofriu, who gave it a more classical aesthetic than the buildings surrounding it. Of particular note is the two-storey bay in the centre of the façade with its arched windows and Italianate columns.

Museu del Perfum / Regia. This perfumery, founded in 1928, apart from offering the finest names in cosmetics and perfumes has a surprise at the back of the shop: a perfume museum that offers an exceptional journey through history via its perfume bottles. Inaugurated in 1961, it is a great museum that is largely unknown to most Barce-

Opening hours: Monday to Friday: 10:30–20h. Saturday: 11–14h. Sunday and holidays closed
Prices: Ticket: 5€ / Reduced ticket: 3€
Information: 932 160 121
www.museudelperfum.com

Bus: 7, 16, 17, 22, 24, 28. Bus Turístic, north and south routes
Metro: L1 (Catalunya), L2 (Passeig de Gràcia), L3 (Catalunya, Passeig de Gràcia), L4 (Passeig de Gràcia)
FGC: (railway) Provença–La Pedrera
Renfe: (railway) Plaça Catalunya, Passeig de Gràcia

lonans. It offers a unique opportunity to admire the more than 5,000 pieces on display which include ancient and modern flasks, miniatures, catalogues, labels and old advertising material.

Pans&Company. A Catalan chain making quality sandwiches at a reasonable price, set up in 1991 in Barcelona.
If you want to eat quickly, it is a good option.

Casa Amatller (1900). Commissioned by the chocolate magnate Antoni Amatller i Costa, who wanted to transform a building from 1875, the architect Josep Puig i Cadafalch came up with a design to give it the appearance of a Gothic urban palace. In this building, modernism combines with Catalan Gothic and some of the urban palaces of the Netherlands, to which are added details of a mediaeval inspiration. The most surprising aspect of the building is its step-shaped upper façade. The sculptural group on the tribune was largely the work of Eusebi Arnau, who was also behind the "St George killing the Dragon" to be found between the two asymmetric doors on the entrance and the representations of animals and people that symbolise the four applied arts: painting, sculp-

ture, architecture and music. The *Casa Amatller* is now a museum that allows visitors to get to know about everyday life for a bourgeois family in Barcelona at the beginning of the 20th Century.

It was declared a National Heritage site in 1976.

🏛 Fundació Institut Amatller d'Art Hispànic.

This entity can be found on the second floor of the building. It was founded by the descendants of the Amatller family and is dedicated to the promotion of (and research into) the history of Hispanic art. It is possible to consult the more than 26,000 volumes in their library, as well as a photographic archive with over half a million historical photographs. The institute's collection includes some 400 glass objects, archaeological remains from the Roman period, Mediaeval and Baroque paintings and sculptures; as well as furniture, examples of liturgical vestments, tapestries and paintings by artists such as Ramon Casas and Lluís Graner, among others.

Price: General ticket: 10€

Information and reservations: 670 466 260
www.casessingulars.com
casessingulars@casessingulars.com

Library: Monday to Friday: 10-15h. Saturday, Sunday and holidays closed
www.amatller.org

Bus: 7, 16, 17, 22, 24, 28. Bus Turístic, north and south routes
Metro: L1 (Catalunya), L2 (Passeig de Gràcia), L3 (Catalunya, Passeig de Gràcia, Diagonal), L4 (Passeig de Gràcia)
FGC: (railway) Provença-La Pedrera
Renfe: (railway) Plaça Catalunya, Passeig de Gràcia

🏛 🏛 **Casa Batlló** (1906). This fabulous house which is said by some to echo a crouching dragon (for others a skull or a carnival costume) was the work of the architectural genius Antoni Gaudí and was commissioned by the textile factory owner Josep Batlló, who wanted to modernise the conventional building built in 1877. Its most spectacular element is its façade, constructed with wrought iron, ceramics, stone and broken-glass mosaics. Gaudí was able to draw on the skills of the best artisans of the time, who helped him to bring to life details such as the balconies in the shape of masks, the dragon's-back roof in tiles of different colours or the pillars and columns on the windows representing bones. A visit to the interior, an expression of sensuality and harmony, is more than recommendable in order to admire the

👜 **Bagués-Masriera.** This is the modernist jeweller's par excellence, with jewellery representing the feminine figure and nature, but also contemporary references. It is located on one of the most exclusive spots on the boulevard. Since 1839, Bagués-Masriera has made pieces that are veritable works of art. Coinciding with the international expansion of the brand, which has even opened a branch in Japan, in 2010 they revamped the building where their original workshop had been (at number 105 on *La Rambla*) and opened the *Hotel boutique Bagués*, which includes a museum with Masriera jewelry collection.

Rear façade of Casa Batlló

decoration. A visit to the terrace and the basement is also a must. There is a cafeteria and a shop with merchandise relating to the building as well as an audio guide service. It is also possible to rent some of the spaces, which can host events of all kinds. It was declared a national heritage site in 1962 and a UNESCO World Heritage site in 2005. **Curious fact:** In 1905, when the French firm *Pathé Frères*, distributors of an innovative product called moving pictures, wished to open a branch in Barcelona, they did so on the ground floor of *Casa Batlló*. When the building was almost finished, in 1907, Pere Milà, the son of Senyor Batlló's business partner, came to visit and admire the work. On being introduced to the architect he assured Gaudí that his next commission would be for him. Neither of them knew it at the time, but they were talking about that Catalan modernist gem the *Casa Milà*, better known as *La Pedrera*.

Opening hours: Monday to Sunday, of 9-21h (last admission 20:20h)

Prices: Adults (+18): 21,50€ / Juniors (7-18): 18,50€ / Student card: 18,50€ / Seniors (+65): 18,50€ / Barcelona province residents: 15€ / Minors (-7): free

Information: 932 160 306
www.casabatllo.es

Bus: 7, 16, 17, 22, 24, 28. Bus Turístic, north and south routes
Metro: L1 (Catalunya), L2 (Passeig de Gràcia), L3 (Catalunya, Passeig de Gràcia, Diagonal), L4 (Passeig de Gràcia)
FGC: (railway) Provença-La Pedrera
Renfe: (railway) Plaça Catalunya, Passeig de Gràcia

Barclays. On the corner of *Passeig de Gràcia* and *Carrer Aragó* is this residential building dating back to 1879; It includes the central offices in Barcelona of this British bank.

Fundació Antoni Tàpies

This is the gallery, cultural centre, archive and headquarters of the foundation dedicated to one of the most important Catalan painters of the 20th Century: Antoni Tàpies (1923–2012). An avant-garde artist, associated with *informalisme*. He created his own means of expression in which tradition and innovation were combined in an abstract style that was full of symbolism, giving great relevance to the underlying basis of the work.

Here it is possible to admire the permanent exhibition of the work of Tàpies, as well as temporary exhibitions. The foundation was created by Tàpies in 1984 in order to promote the study and knowledge of modern and contemporary art, as well as combining the organisation of temporary exhibitions, symposia, conferences and cinema cycles with the publishing of books and articles accompanying the activities and periodic events dedicated to the great Catalan artist.

The collection mainly comprises paintings, sculptures, drawings, books and engravings which demonstrate the different artistic facets of Tàpies, as well as the different typologies, techniques and materials that he used during his career.

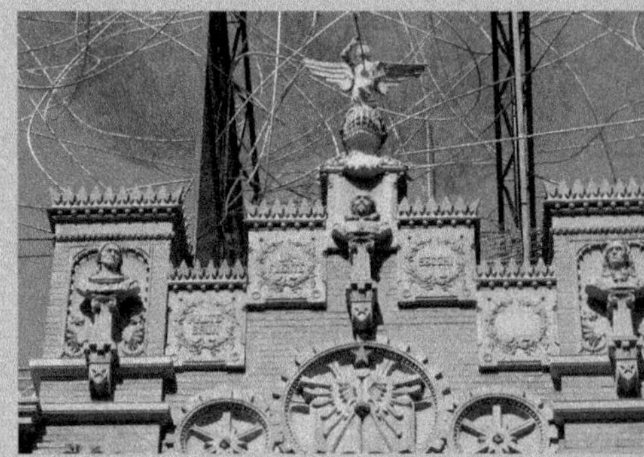

The foundation's building

1879: The publisher Ramon Montaner commissioned his nephew, Lluís Domènech i Montaner (1849-1923) to construct a building for his publishing house: Montaner i Simon. The building became one of the first examples of architectural modernism in Barcelona. It was the first to integrate open brick and iron work, which, thanks to

their strength and lightness, allow for the creation of bigger and freer floors. Although the materials used were eminently industrial, the structure of the building is that of a palace, with its central impluvium. The façade incorporated a number of symbolic elements emphasising the industrial modernity of the publishing house. When the publishers closed in 1981, Antoni Tàpies visited the building and saw the great potential it had for his Antoni Tàpies Foundation project.

1986–1990: Work on reforming and conditioning the building was carried out under the direction of Roser Amadó and Lluís Domènech Girbau. In order to raise the height of the building, which had become somewhat trapped between the imposing walls of the buildings on either side, as well as to stress

its new identity, Antoni Tàpies came up with the idea of a sculpture to crown the building, *Núvol i cadira* (cloud and chair). It was installed in 1990 and was the result of a technical collaboration with Pere Casanovas. It caused a storm among the general public.

The new head office of the foundation was opened in June 1990.

2008–2010: The architectural firm Ábalos+Sentkiewicz carried out a second reform of the building to bring it into line with current accessibility regulations and to recover much of its original industrial character. On this occasion, Tàpies' work *Mitjó* ("Sock", scale model, 1991; final work, 2010) was installed on the terrace of the foundation, above the new office buildings.

Carrer Aragó towards the River Llobregat

≋

Aragó, 272

⌂ **Servei Estació.** Entering this building is a chromatic festival for the eyes and a tactile delight for the hands. It is a historic shop in the centre of the city, which opened, in 1928, under the name "Service Station", as a place to buy petrol and a shop for spare parts and services for automobiles. During the civil war it was collectivised, then under the dictatorship of General Franco its name had to be hispanicised into *Servicio Estación*. In the decade of the 1950s and 60s, the company diversified and introduced bicycles, motorcycles and hardware. It has evolved until it has become *the* place to look for materials and DIY solutions, as well as anything related with decoration and design for the home or business and commercial spaces. The last major overhaul, in 2010, modernised the whole shop and won the City Council's prize for the Best Commercial Establishment in the city. It continues to offer all kinds of plastics, wood, cork, methacrylates, rugs or oilcloths to those who need them, or simply to those who enjoy wandering around its Aladdin's cave of infinite shapes and colours. On the second floor you can access the patio from where you can see the rear façades of *Casa Batlló, Casa Amatller* and, further away, the *Casa Lleó Morera.*

⋀

Aragó, 261

🍴 **Mussol.** Restaurant where you can enjoy Catalan cuisine with specialities such as in-season vegetables and meats prepared to traditional recipes.

Aragó, 255

🏛 **Fundació Antoni Tàpies.** See the "Of particular note" section, pages 48-49.

From Aragó to València

47

Desigual. Has carved out a niche for itself in the Spanish and International markets through often polemical publicity campaigns. It offers clothes of a very informal and colourful nature that fill many a wardrobe.

Max & Co. This is the more affordable brand of the Max Mara company. It offers day-to-day wear for the elegant urban woman, with neat and marked outlines inspired by Italian couture. Look out for the furniture that decorates this boutique and gives it a real 1950s feel.

49

 **Sisley.** This is the haute-couture branch of United Colors of Benetton. They have urbane and informal, but elegant, collections; along with all the necessary accessories.

Hackett. This is a British brand that invites their customers, both adults and children, to dress as English gentleman. The store has some 320 m^2 of space spread over two floors. It is decorated in dark woods, carpets and low lighting, all of which gives the place an air of seriousness. It has changing rooms with a privileged view of the *Passeig*.

 **Lacoste.** This is one of the most iconic of all brands. Founded in 1933 by French tennis champion René Lacoste, who invented the polo neck that is still the flagship of the brand; their items have a crocodile embroidered onto them because that was the nickname that sports journalists of the time had given to Lacoste. Today the store sells sportswear for men, women and children, as well as footwear, colognes and all kinds of accessories. **Curious fact:** the low reliefs which can be seen on either side of the entrance are the work of the important Catalan sculptor Frederic Marès and are titled *El treball* (work). They were created in 1950 for a former branch of the *Banco Hispano Americano*.

Rocamora Apartments. These are ideal for those visitors who wish to experience life as lived in the stately apartments of the *Eixample*, with their mouldings, hydraulic mosaics and a traditional lift.

 **Liu Jo.** This Italian brand belongs to the brothers Marco and Vannis Marchi. Since 2012, they have been offering women their refined and glamorous lines of clothes, shoes and accessories, as well as an exclusive range for children.

 **Puma.** This is the shop for fans of limited edition sports shoes. It also sells sports clothes and accessories.

Bulevard Rosa. A Shopping Mall with two entrances on the *Passeig de Gràcia* (also on numbers 55-57), two more on the street running parallel, the *Rambla de Catalunya*, and two more on *Aragó* and *València*. It

contains more than sixty boutiques dedicated to fashion, cosmetics, footwear, jewellery, accessories and even foodstuffs, as well as cafes and restaurants.

Curious fact: on this spot once stood one of the most elegant cafe-restaurants in the city: the *Salón Rosa*. Opened in 1932, it was a meeting point for Barcelona's high society until 1974 when the building was demolished.

Fishop. Restaurant for lovers of fish and seafood, whether Mediterranean or Japanese. Go down some stairs to choose your fresh fish, which can be sampled in the basement or at one of the tables outside on the avenue.

Publi building (1977). This white office block with its irregular sized oval windows, giving it the air of a spaceship, is the work of the architect Josep M. Fargas Falp.

Nespresso. This well-known brand of coffee offers capsules with a wide range of tastes and aromas for anyone who owns one of their coffee machines so that they can enjoy the best espresso without leaving home.

Bulevard dels Antiquaris. Climbing the stairs you reach a group of shops selling antiques and collector's items that will keep fans of this type of furniture and these objects entertained for hours.

Orogold Cosmetics. A small establishment specialising in cosmetic products manufactured with particles of 24 carat colloidal gold. The secret of their cosmetics is the purity of the gold.

Bimba y Lola. While the shop window is on the *Passeig*, a stair leads down to the rest of the shop which is in the basement. This is a Spanish fashion brand created in 2005 by the sisters María and Uxía Domínguez. They offer a comprehensive collection of textiles and fashion items, with original designs and unique prints using a singular selection of materials, finishes, colours and outlines.

Furla. From their origins in a small Italian village outside Bologna, the Furlanetto family have been making simple and beautiful bags for women since 1927. Simplicity and beauty also dominate the decoration in this shop, in which the chromatic and spatial distribution of the bags is the main attraction.

Rabat Flash. With a structure that echoes the modernist pharmacy *Martí Lledó* that once stood here, this is one of the two branches that this jewellery brand has on *Passeig de Gràcia* (the other is that number 99). They also specialise in deluxe watches. During your visit, take a moment to admire the furniture left over from the former pharmacy.

Carrer València towards the River Llobregat

València, 272

Magerit. This is the flagship store of the jeweller's Ramón Jiménez Barbara, founded in 1994. Of particular note is the store's especially elegant decoration. The name of the jewellers is the old Arab name for the city of Madrid, from which the brand originally came.

València, 249

Miu Sushi. This is a branch of a chain of restaurants in Barcelona offering classic Japanese cuisine of a more than reasonable quality at very affordable prices. Go downstairs to access the restaurant's dining room, which is decorated with a binomial combination of turquoise-white, wood and large Asian lamps.

A Birds-Eye view: the terraces

When it is fine weather, normally from May to October, many hotels and buildings in Barcelona *(Passeig de Gràcia* included) offer visitors the chance to enjoy the city from a privileged position. Day or night, the *Hotel Condes* (with its *Terrassa Alaire)* the *Hotel Casa Fuster* (the Blue View), at the top of the boulevard, the Majestic & Spa (La Dolce Vitae), the Mandarin Oriental, or the hotels Royal Passeig de Gràcia, Omm, Índigo, as well as the Renaissance Barcelona Hotel, the Gallery Hotel or the Catalunya Plaza (H10) open their terraces to those who crave a bird's eye view of the *Passeig de Gràcia* and Barcelona. Other establishments offer a good viewing platform for the city, such as the terraces of the *Suites Av-*

enue Luxe apartments, the department store *El Corte Inglés* in *Plaça Catalunya* or, most especially, the terrace of *La Pedrera* on summer nights, which often has musical concerts programmed. In all cases, it is not necessary to be a guest at the hotel to enjoy a drink or a meal with a view there. In addition, if you visit the city during the month of June, you could participate in the **Setmana de les Terrasses dels Hotels de Barcelona,** organized by the Hotel Guild of Barcelona, in which some 60 establishments offer parties, performances, workshops, exhibitions, activities for children, gastronomic surprises and live music on their terraces.

Barcelona Shopping Night

Inspired by the Fashion Night Out in New York (brainchild of the all-powerful director of *Vogue*, Ana Wintour) the Barcelona Shopping Night has transformed the *Passeig de Gràcia* into an ideal setting for an extraordinary evening out since 2010. The traffic is halted and more than eighty boutiques open their doors, setting up stalls outside with fashion exhibitions, food and drink tastings, all kinds of shows and even photo calls so that everyone can feel a star for the day. Needless to say, there are also important discounts catering for a public eager to sample great prices, as well as a unique experience. Strolling around, daydreaming and shopping: the three activities which make *Passeig de Gràcia* the authentic heart of the city of Barcelona - now available at night.

Some of the activities you can participate in during this special evening include posing before the illustrators of the European Institute of Design, who will draw a *look* that fits the profile and fashion sense of the "model for a night" before them. You can also taste products personalised by the most prestigious chefs such as Carme Ruscalleda or Martín Berasategui; have a haircut for charity, take part in a thousand and one raffles of beauty products or for grants for studying fashion at the finest academies in the city. If you are even luckier, you could attend the themed party, held a few days before, at the *Palau de la Virreina* on *La Rambla*, which kicks off the celebrations. In 2013, in commemoration of 200 years since the birth of Wagner, the theme used to decorate the entire palace was Valhalla, named after one of the German maestro's compositions. That same year, Barcelona Shopping Night received more than 60,000 visitors.

From València to Mallorca

 **Guess.** One of the two boutiques this originally American brand has on the *Passeig* (the other is at number 13). This is the store for those with a youthful, sensual and adventurous lifestyle. They have a complete line of clothing and accessories for men, women and children, as well as lingerie, perfumes and gifts.

 **Casas Jofre** (1910). This building was a commission by the siblings Josefa and Alexandre Jofre to the architect Bonaventura Bassegoda Amigó, who proposed a façade which would unite the two houses. Note the two higher sides, reminiscent of towers, crowned with floral designs and the date 1906, despite the fact that the building was not finished until four years later.

 **Mango.** This is the well-known brand started in 1984 by the Catalan businessmen, of Turkish extract, Isak Andic. Since then, the company has expanded into more than 100 countries in which it has nearly 2000 sales points, one of which is this clothes and accessories boutique for women.

Uterqüe. This accessories boutique, opened in 2008, has a clear premise: to make accessories a basic element in a woman's wardrobe. By accessories they mean things like jewellery, scarves, leather goods, belts, sunglasses, gloves and shoes.

67

Oysho. This is a chain of boutiques selling modern and comfortable underwear at affordable prices. This branch, due to its location and design, is one of the most attractive in the chain. Its slate floors, its decoration with oriental touches and its setting in a 19th Century building make it exceptional.

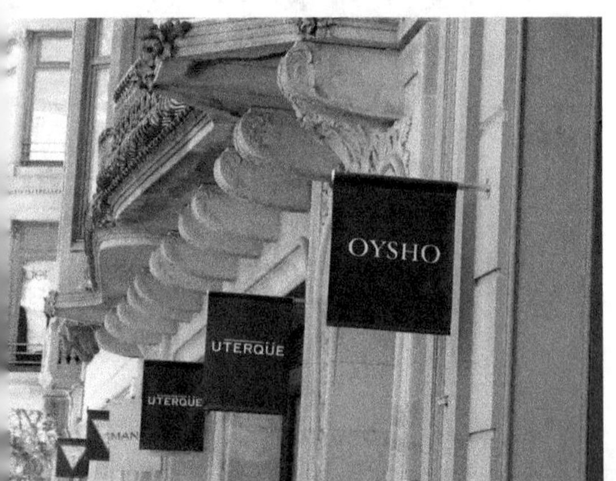

Tru Trussardi. This is the youthful, urban and casual line of the emblematic brand of gloves Dante Trussardi, founded in Bergamo in 1911. Since 2005, they have staked out their place on the avenue thanks to a fashion concept that, while not revolutionary, is very effective. Collections for men, women and children in a chic style that is both elegant and functional.

69

 **Majestic Residence.** In 2011, the Majestic Hotel Group remodelled this building into luxury tourist apartments for longer stays, or for families. There are 28 of them, with sizes ranging between 90 and 170 m^2.

United Colors of Benetton. The world-famous Italian brand of multi-coloured informal clothes also

has a boutique on the *Passeig de Gràcia*, complete with its name in neon lights.

 **71**

🛍 **Escada Sport.** This German haute-couture brand (which you can find at number 79) has diversified and opened this lower-priced line that is equally chic.

Curious fact: If you stand on the pavement outside the building and look up at the rooftop terrace, you can see a metal dome which from 1953 to 2005 was the observatory of the **Agrupació Astronòmica de Barcelona, Aster.** Back then, from *Passeig de Gràcia* you could reach out to the stars.

🍴 **Moncho's.** A classic Barcelona restaurant, having thirteen establishments specialising in fish and seafood. Dishes and tapas can be sampled on the outdoor terrace or in the interior. Uninterrupted cooking from 11:00 am to 01:00 am the next day.

 **73**

🏢 **Condes de Barcelona** (5*). With 126 rooms, an outdoor swimming pool, a solarium and salons for

various events, this is one of the most illustrious hotels on the boulevard. The restaurant is supervised by the Basque chef Martín Berasategui, who runs the restaurant annex, the *Loidi*. Access is also available to the *Terrassa Alaire*, an exceptionally located cocktail bar.

La Perla. This brand of deluxe Italian lingerie has its second branch in the city here, with premises extending to 250 m^2. It sells exquisite collections of lingerie, swimwear, shoes and pyjamas. It also sells men's underwear and swimwear.

Zadig & Voltaire. A fashion firm owned by Thierry Gallier, with a very Parisian spirit and a *rock chic* style aimed at daring people: tights, black leather, metallised fabrics, boots and their infamous skulls.

Carrer Mallorca Mallorca towards the River Llobregat

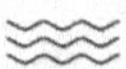

Mallorca, 248-250

Loidi. This is a restaurant run by the prestigious Basque chef Martín Berasategui. At the bar you can try some exquisite dishes or tapas at a price far below that of eating at table.

Terraza Alaire. This is a gastronomic and musical proposition on the eighth floor of the *Hotel Condes de Barcelona* with magnificent views of the *Pedrera* and the *Sagrada Família* and a selection of cocktails, tapas and sandwiches.

Mallorca, 246

🛍 **Jordi Forcada Groceries.** One of the last strongholds of traditional commerce in the district, it was founded in 1875 by Josep Forcada i Davi and was the precedent for today's supermarkets. This grocer's is still run by the fourth generation of the family who started it. It has provided food for the grand homes on the *Passeig de Gràcia* and the *Rambla de Catalunya* for over 100 years.

Mallorca, 259

🍴 **Lasarte.** A restaurant situated on the elegant ground floor of the Casa Enric Batlló, which forms part of the *Hotel Condes de Barcelona*, but is open to the public. Closed for renovations during the period 2014-2015.

Mallorca, 253-257

🏛 **Casa Ángel Batlló.** A group of three buildings encompassing the same façade; they were built in 1896, for one of the Batlló family, and were designed by the Catalan architect Josep Vilaseca i Casanovas. The façade consists of six identical sections, crowned with a pointed arch on columns which link up horizontally with the balconies on the first floor and above. The interior of the arches and the pilasters separating the six sections are decorated with elegantly floral engravings.

Mallorca, 251

🏢 **Alexandra Barcelona a Double Tree by Hilton** (4*). A hotel with a functional, welcoming and modern design which has taken great care of every detail. It has four large salons available for events.

🍴 **Da Luca.** A Genovese restaurant, specialising in Italian cuisine from the Liguria region; it offers tradition and culinary excellence.

Santa Eulalia, the oldest fashion boutique in the city

This is the temple of traditional Barcelona boutiques. In 1843, Domingo Taberner Prims opened the first *Santa Eulalia* boutique; named after the patron saint of Barcelona. This first establishment was on the *Rambla* at the *Pla de la Boqueria* and was where the first high fashion show in the city was held in 1926. In 1941, the company opened a new branch at number 60 of the *Passeig de Gràcia.* In 1944, the company owned the shop on the Rambla and also opened another for men only at their current home of Passeig de Gràcia, 93. In the 1960s

The Santa Eulalia store at the Pla de la Boqueria in 1920

business expanded and the first *prêt-à-porter* collections were displayed in fashion shows in the boutique. They were so successful that the formula was exported to New York and the Moroccan city of Tangier. In 1995, there was the last high fashion show at the boutique shop. From 2006 onwards, the company rebranded itself with designer *prêt-à-porter* fashion collections for women. After a remodelling carried out by the American architect William Sofield, the new *Santa Eulalia* opened in 2011 as a cosmopolitan establishment full of tradition and well worth a visit.

Every element at *Santa Eulalia* is a feast for the eyes, right down to their *art déco* logo created in 1926. Occupying more than 2,000 m², the build-

Santa Eulalia building on Passeig de Gràcia, 60, in 1941

is actually from the first *Santa Eulàlia* establishment on the *Pla de la Boqueria*. Parts of the 1920s lifts have been used, as well as art deco chairs and counters. Display cabinets and the oaken staircase are from the former store at *Passeig de Gràcia*, 60. In the cafeteria, the counter is from an old bar in Toulouse, the Thonet chairs are upholstered with a reprint of a historic Liberty print and the serigraphed marble tables have wrought iron feet. On the rooftop garden terrace, the metal Tolix chairs are made to a design from 1927. Not everything is a reproduction, however, take special note of the two Barcelona model chairs upholstered in yellow at the entrance, as well as the enormous suspended glass lamps on the façade, designed by Miguel Milà. In all, a visual feast and unforgettable experience.

ing has a restaurant, cafeteria and an outdoor terrace on the top floor, along with a *pop-up store* and spacious display areas for collections for both men and women.

A visit to ground floor, where you can admire the work of the tailors, who measure clients for made-to-measure shirts and trousers, is a must. Stop for a moment and take note of the cardboard patterns reserved for each client and classified alphabetically. Among its display cabinets, bevelled mirrors and retro-styled counters, the upper floor reveals plush sofas upholstered in velvet.

The research behind the recapturing of the boutique's historic tradition has been painstaking: part of the furniture

Provença

From Mallorca
to Provença

Numbers 75-87

Mallorca

 **Casa Enric Batlló** (1896). Designed by the Catalan architect Josep Vilaseca i Casanovas, it is a manor house that combines brick with stone and ceramic panels. The main floor has a very elegant exterior gallery with ornate details using stone and medallions with heraldic motifs, in addition to the decorations on the lower balcony, in ceramics. The decorative wrought iron railings on the façade were designed by the architect Lluís Domènech i Montaner. The upper terrace, which has a small swimming pool, is open

to the public and offers stunning views of *Passeig de Gracia*. (During the period 2014-2015, the building is closed for the refurbishment of the *Hotel Condes de Barcelona*, but will reopen as a luxury five-star hotel.) Lit up at night, the brickwork facade is especially graceful.

Curious fact: If you are a literary buff, take a good look at the customers you might find in the restaurant, the coffee bar or the hotel lobby, because, if you're lucky, they might be writers like Paul Auster or Martin Amis, their Spanish publishers *Anagrama* always put guests up in this hotel.

Tous. This is one of their two jeweller's on the *Passeig* (the other is at number 18). Founded in 1920, with its head offices in Manresa, it is the official agent for Rolex watches, as well as offering their own renowned jewels, bags and accessories.

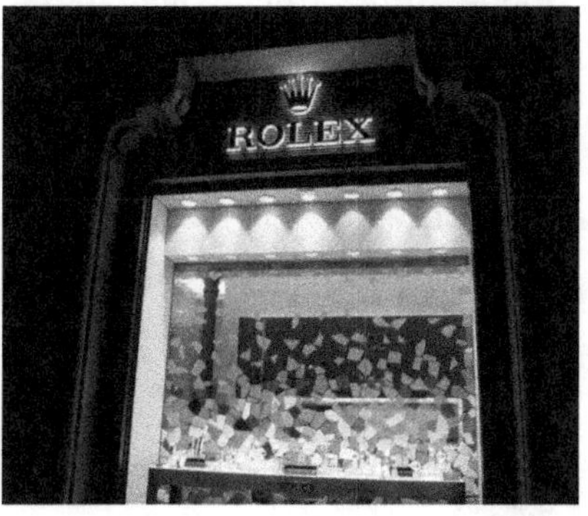

Novecento. A jeweller's specialising in antique jewellery and in buying and selling gold.

Casa Josep Borràs (1925). The central section which stands out and forms four galleries (the lower one framed by two sculpted tablets and the upper two by two pairs of columns with Corinthian capitals) is the result of a modification carried out by the architect Francesc de Paula Nebot, who also added the top floor.

Hermès. With 254 boutiques around the world, the company was founded in Paris in 1837 as a shop for horse riding equipment. It is still run by descendents of the Hermès family. They are proud of having all of their leather bags handmade by craftsmen, producing luxury that shuns ostentation. Here you can admire two of their most celebrated creations: the Birkin and Kelly bags, named in honour of the actresses Jane Birkin and Grace Kelly. There is also a wide selection of famous perfumes, ties, handkerchiefs, watches and jewellery. It is worth taking a long look at their shop window which is usually very special.

accessories for women who wish to enjoy elegance and glamour.

Karen Millen. A British brand, started in 1981, it has been on the *Passeig de Gràcia* since 2010 with this boutique which combines silver and glass. Urban and functional fashion, accessories and shoes for women, with a touch of glamour.

79

 A singular building with a blue façade that brings together two shops:

Escada. An idea that, since 1976, has triumphed all over the world: the chic in *haute-couture* can also be democratised, or least an attempt can be made to do so. The Germans, Margaretha and Wolfgang Ley founded the business, but then moved on. The brand has since widened its scope with the appearance of *Escada Sport*, but the original spirit of "sophisticated luxury and joyful escapism" which came to define the brand is still maintained as their logo. Clothes and

81

 **Stuart Weitzman.** A shoe shop named after the German designer. It is one of the top luxury brands in the world, with boutiques in Milan, New York and Paris, among other cities. Their daring runs to all kinds of materials (cork, plastic, vinyl and wallpaper, but also 24 carat gold). They have even designed a line of *elegant espadrilles*, which allows you to buy a reinvention of the mythical "camping shoes" for €315; there has never been such a high price on nostalgia. For the shop in Barcelona, in

a resplendent white, the decorators have created a space that echoes *La Pedrera*, with undulations along the walls.

 83

Suites Avenue Luxe (2009). The spectacular façade in rippling aluminium that covers this luxury apartment building is the work of the prestigious Japanese architect Toyo Ito. The building is in dialogue with *La Pedrera*, on the opposite side of the *Passeig de Gràcia*, Indeed, the view of the Gaudí building from inside the apartments is spectacular. There are 41 apartments ideal for mid to long-term occupation. The building has a gym, a sauna, outdoor swimming pools, a solarium, a community terrace, conference rooms, a car park and even a museum showing works of Hindu and Buddhist art. **Curious fact:** until its remodelling, in 2008, this was where the *Europa* Company had its offices. The building was constructed in 1962, after the demolition of the modernist *Viuda Almirall* house.

⌂ **Hugo Boss.** The brand started life in 1924, in a village in Germany, as a small clothes shop for men. It has since become world-renowned for its clothes for young male and female executives, who can also find weekend-wear here. This is the company's main boutique in Barcelona and has sections for men and women spread over two floors. Colognes and perfumes, which were introduced in 1984, have given a new thrust to the brand and are well represented here through classics such as Boss Bottled or Hugo: Hugo Boss. Their advertising slogan sums up the spirit of the brand: "I don't expect success, I prepare for it."

85

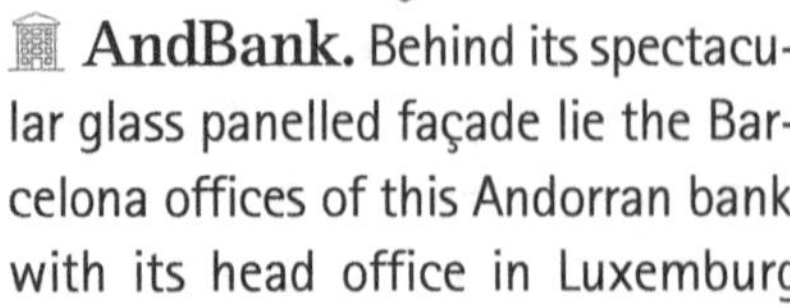

🏛 **AndBank.** Behind its spectacular glass panelled façade lie the Barcelona offices of this Andorran bank, with its head office in Luxemburg since 2010.

87

⌂ **Carolina Herrera.** On the corner with *Carrer Provença*, a number of red awnings with the well-known initials CH shade the shop windows of the boutique of this Venezuelan designer, who now lives in New York. On sale are dresses, trousers, T-shirts, sweaters, jackets, shoes, exclusive perfumes, sunglasses, bags, jewellery and handkerchiefs with personality.

⌂ **Circa.** The attic of this building, with its views of *La Pedrera* convinced this New York based jeweller's to open out to the European market in Barcelona, in 2012, rather than in Milan or Madrid. The secret of their success has been offering an exclusive and discreet atmosphere to those who possess jewellery that, for one reason or another, they wish to get rid of. It is the ideal place and setting to carry out this type of operation.

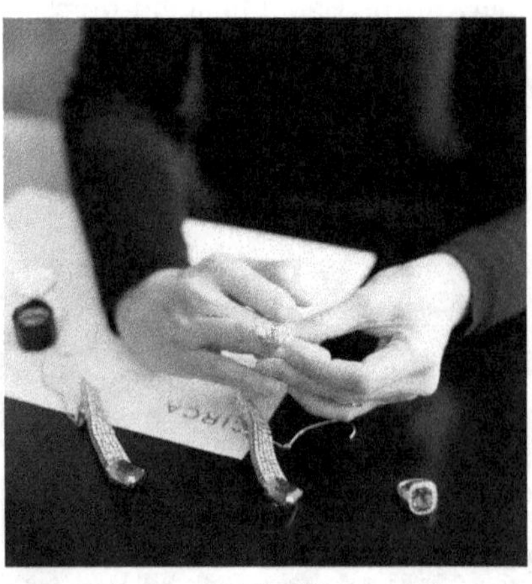

Carrer Provença towards the River Llobregat

Curious fact: *Carrer Provença* was the old border between Barcelona and the village of *Gràcia* and on the crossroads with *Passeig de Gràcia* there was a tollbooth which collected taxes on certain goods entering the city. It was here, in 1830 that the Ceres Fountain was installed, which today can be found on the viewing point *(Mirador del Llobregat)* on the mountain of Montjuïc.

≈≈≈

Provença, 292

 **Purificación García.** In 2011, the designer Purificación García opened a boutique here with more than 300 m² of space. It sells clothes and accessories for men, while for women it offers a space where the sobriety and good taste characteristic of this brand reigns.

Provença, 290

Magnolia Antic. Dresses by Hermès, Chanel and Pedro Rod-

ríguez, hats and headdresses from the 1940s, rigid bags from the 1930s, or 18th C. English porcelain are just some of the magic objects that Tatiana Almagro has on offer in this unique corner of the city. The shop is somewhat hidden down in the left-hand semi-basement of this imposing building, but before going down to it be sure to admire the staircase leading to the upper floors.

Cortana. In the right-hand semi-basement there is the boutique of the Mallorcan designer Rosa Esteva, winner of the *T de Telva* award for the best Spanish designer in 2012. On display are sober and elegant collections for women.

Provença, 288-286

El Principal. One of the restaurants with the most authentic atmospheres on the *Passeig de Grà-*

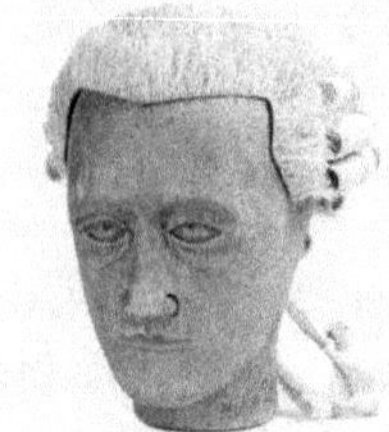

cia: an enclave on the main floor of a stately building on the *Eixample*. It is worth a visit to the rear garden, where you can also eat. There are set menus for lunch during the week and at the weekend. Salons can be hired for banquets and celebrations.

Provença, 284-282

🛍 **Institute Saurina.** A beauty centre occupying more than 1300 m², distributed over three floors and with 19 booths for facial and corporal treatments. It includes an area for aesthetic medicine, the Saurina Clinic.

Rambla de Catalunya, 99

🏛 **Museu de la Perruqueria Raffel Pagés.** This is the place to get to know the world of hairdressing and personal image throughout history, in both its everyday and artistic expressions. Objects for personal use, crafts, professional tools, jars, prints, photographs, toys, publications, documents and so on, form part of the 4,000 pieces on display in the museum's collection. A visit begins in Mesopotamia, takes in the cultures of Egypt, Greece and Rome, illustrates the Middle Ages and demonstrates the public affirmation of the hairdresser in Europe from the 18th Century onwards. Finally it brings us into the modern era when, in the 20th Century, a whole industry developed linked to hairdressing and hair care.

△△

Opening hours: Monday to Friday: 9-18h. Saturdays: 9-13h

Prices Prices (with guided visit): Individual: 7,50 € / Groups: 3,50 €

Information and reservations: 932 052 419
museum@raffelpages.com
www.museumraffelpages.com

Bus: 7,16,17, 22, 24, V17, H10
Metro: L3, L5 (Diagonal)
FGC: (railway) Provença–La Pedrera
Renfe: (railway) Passeig de Gràcia

Provença, 241

🍴 **Mauri.** This establishment, with its modernist decoration, is one of the best cake shops in the city. It was started in 1929 by Francesc Mauri. It also offers a cafeteria service, a restaurant, takeaway food, cold cuts and a salad bar. It is on the corner of that other great city avenue, parallel to the *Passeig de Gràcia*, the *Rambla de Catalunya*.

From Provença to Rosselló

Numbers 89-99

89

🛍 **Hoss Intropia.** Colourful Spanish fashion for women. Since 1994, they have opened boutiques in more than 40 countries.

🛍 **Anna Mora.** The Catalan dressmaker offers clothes for today's women.

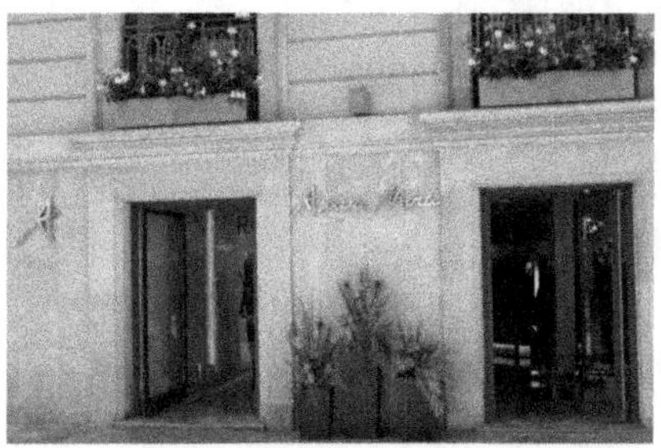

🛍 **Ernest Oriol.** On the first floor, beneath navy blue awnings with golden letters, lies this small jewellers which guarantees a huge difference between it and other jewellers in that the whole process, from the selection of stones to the manufacture and sale are directly supervised by the company. Since 1951, they have produced exclusive, quality jewellery served in an atmosphere that successfully reproduces that of a bourgeois household: carpeted floors, tables and chairs, a striking traditional entrance and windows with views of *La Pedrera*.

91

🛍 **Ermenegildo Zegna.** The rectangular metal knobs used to open the double doors of this emblematic branch of this swish Italian tailor's, inaugurated in 2013, perfectly matches the elegance of the brand. The shop takes up 360 m^2, spread over three floors and is dedicated to Zegna collections for every occasion: shoes, bags, colognes and accesso-

ries. On the upper floor there is the *VIP Couture* section, with private salons decorated in wood and a terrace.

🛍 **Galería Loewe.** This is one of the two shops on the *Passeig* (the first is at number 35) representing this Spanish brand of leather bags and silk handkerchiefs. It opened in 2014.

93

🛍 **Santa Eulalia.** See the "Of particular note" section, pages 62-63.

Passatge de la Concepció

To access this passageway you must pass under an ornate metal sign painted green. Along the passage, you will find a number of highly recommendable restaurants and bars. At the end you will find yourself in the *Rambla de Catalunya*, the other great imposing avenue running parallel with *Passeig de Gràcia*. It has a wide central pedestrian area with trees and a number of terraces where you can eat.

P. de la Concepció, 2
🍴 **Sushi Shop.** A Japanese takeaway restaurant.

P. de la Concepció, 5
🍴 **El Japonés.** Under a cascade of green you will find the entrance to this Japanese restaurant with long tables for sharing the experience and a youthful ambience.

95

 **Dolce & Gabbana.** Double glass doors for this double-barrelled store, founded in 1985 under the auspices of Domenico Dolce and Stefano Gabbana, who dress global stars such as Madonna, Lady Gaga, Monica Bellucchi or Britney Spears. They have been defined as the inheritors of the mantle (for the noughties) that had belonged to Armani in the 1980s or Prada in the 1990s; that of being the great Italian stylists who everyone wanted to imitate. Black dominates the decoration of their establishment and two enormous statues of an oriental inspiration receive shoppers looking for clothes, accessories, perfumes, make up, jewellery, watches and even mobile phones.

P. de la Concepció, 5

Tragaluz. Traditional Barcelonan cuisine, but with avant-garde touches in a charismatic site with a retractable ceiling allowing you to eat under the stars.

P. de la Concepció, 7-9

ⓘ **Turisme de Barcelona.** The head offices of the city's tourist board, here you can find maps, postcards, information and suggestions that will help you get to know Barcelona.

Opening hours: daily: 8-20h
Closed: 1st of January and 25th of December
Information: 932 853 834
info@barcelonaturisme.com
www.barcelonaturisme.com

Bus: 7, 16, 17, 22, 24, V17, 39
Metro: L3, L5 (Diagonal)
FGC: (railway) Provença-La Pedrera
Renfe: (railway) Passeig de Gràcia

P. de la Concepció, 10

Mordisco. A classic city eating house specialising in healthy Mediterranean cuisine. Low-calorie takeaway food is also available. It is a family concern that started in 1987.

P. de la Concepció, 12

Boca Grande. A restaurant with excellent seafood that has a cocktail bar annex, the **Boca Chica**; sophisticated decoration and a lovely terrace on the upper floor.

97

🛍 **Jimmy Choo.** With more than 150 stores throughout the world, this British Shoe brand, founded by Tamara Mellon has a place on the podium of the most exclusive brands, with distinctive clients such as Hollywood stars. Their shoes are sexy and manufactured in an Italian style, but they also sell bags and accessories. This store, with its 114 m², has furniture in transparent plastic and the dominant colour is a dazzling white.

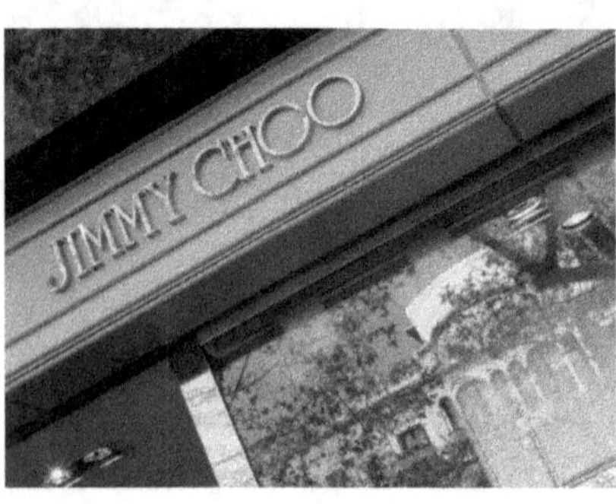

🍴 **Starbucks.** The most famous coffee shop chain in the Western world, which now has 20 establishments in Barcelona, offers a long list of coffees which can be sipped on the sofas indoors, or on the terrace outside.

99

🛍 **Montblanc.** Beneath an apartment block with a façade in brown and white squares (refurbished in 2009 by the architectural studio OAB) is a boutique of this classic German make of items for writing. With 300 m² on two floors, today it is an icon for luxury articles: watches, jewellery, eyeglasses and perfumes, among others.

Curious fact: The name of the fabled Montblanc pens dates back to 1910. During a card game, one of the relatives of the family who founded the company compared the perfection of the pen with that of the highest mountain in the Alps.

🛍 **Rabat.** Veteran Catalan jeweller's, with an exhibition of exclusive designs. They are also distributors for the highest quality watches.

🛍 **Dirk Bikkembergs.** The boutique of this Belgian designer of sports clothing. The shop takes up some 600 m² distributed over two floors and is the ideal space for men who consider themselves dynamic, refined, sporty and cool. Take special note of the football shaped table legs.

Carrer Rosselló towards the River Llobregat

Rosselló, 255

Nello's Bar. A New York style hamburger joint with innovative ingredients such as pork from Segovia or angler fish, as well as a wide assortment of beers, wines and gin tonics.

Rosselló, 249

Gallery Hotel (4*). An iron and glass canopy marks the entrance to the hotel, which has a swimming pool and a terrace known as "The Top" (open from April to November), conference rooms and 110 guest rooms offering every comfort.

El Café del Gallery. What looks like a gallery running along the side of the Hotel Gallery is, in fact, a café and restaurant serving Mediterranean cuisine (with fresh locally-produced products). It is nice and quiet, and has an open air terrace in the interior. The series of lamps hanging from the ceiling give it a special atmosphere.

From Rosselló
to the Diagonal

Numbers 101–107

 Marella. Italian fashion for women of a dynamic and contemporary spirit. Colourful and glamorous designs complemented with excellent quality handbags and footwear.

 Samoa. A classic city eating house. It opened as a pizzeria in 1962, but now has a wider ranging menu, which includes items from the delicatessen such as oysters in white wine. It also has outdoor tables.

 Lladró. This two-storey store allows shoppers to admire every detail of the world-famous Lladró porcelain figures. Each one is handmade in the village of Almàssera, near Valencia. Since 1953, when the Lladró brothers began making porcelain figures inspired by 18th Century styles, the growth of the brand has been exponential and is very healthy today. They have stores all over the world and new lines such as their lighting and decoration for bathrooms. Take a moment to admire the lamp hanging over the staircase to the upper floor as well as some of the unique oriental style pieces on show. The brand is beginning to make its mark in emerging markets, such as China or India. Lladró is present in the world's most important cities with the Lladró Boutiques.

 **Carrera y Carrera.** Jeweller's, founded in Madrid in 1885, by a family of jewellery makers with a long tradition. It is now one of the most prestigious names in the world. Their distinctiveness lies in the originality of their pieces, of a very Spanish inspiration, with volume and full of symbolism.

103

 **Imaginarium.** This kids' shop had the brilliant idea of offering an alternative door for boys and girls under which only they could comfortably pass and which delights every child who tries it. On sale inside are toys and costumes for young children.

105

 **Conselleria d'Empresa i Ocupació.** The offices of the Employers and Employment Department of the Catalan Government.

107

 **Robert Palace** (1903). See the "Of particular note" section, pages 78-79.

103

The oak on Passeig de Gràcia. This was the title of a prose piece that the Catalan poet and priest Mossèn Cinto Verdaguer published in 1903 as a homage to a holm oak tree that grew on the sidewalk of the avenue, a silent witness to the woods that had once extended over the Barcelona plane. The city council had it chopped down in 1908, apparently because it was an obstacle for the trams. Today, on the same site, it has been replaced with a new tree and an inscription on the ground with a fragment of the Verdaguer text: "Indomitable Almogàver! Old trouper, do you know how to get in line with this company of new and polished plane trees; in their Sunday best and overweening?"

The Palau Robert (1903)

This neoclassical styled palace was built for the Marquis and Count Robert Robert i Surís (Barcelona 1851-*Torroella de Montgrí* 1929), an influential financier, politician and aristocrat who had bought the plot on the junction between *Passeig de Gràcia* and the *Diagonal* from the Marquis of Salamanca. Robert had a number of existing single-family bungalows demolished in order to build his private residence there. Far from the modernist spirit of the moment, he commissioned the French architect Henry Grandpierre, who had worked on the Universal Exposition of 1900 in Paris. He, in turn, chose the Catalan architect Joan Martorell i Montells to supervise the work. The garden was designed by the municipal gardener Ramon Oliva, who would later take charge of the vegetation in *Plaça Catalunya*. The decorative palms came from the Universal Exposition in Barcelona in 1888. With the outbreak of the Civil War in 1936, the building passed into the hands of the Catalan government the *Generalitat de Catalunya* who made it the head offices of the Council for Culture. However this represented a mere parenthesis because after the war the building was given back to the Robert family. During later years it changed hands several times until finally it was owned by the Banc Central until 1981 when, once again, it was acquired by

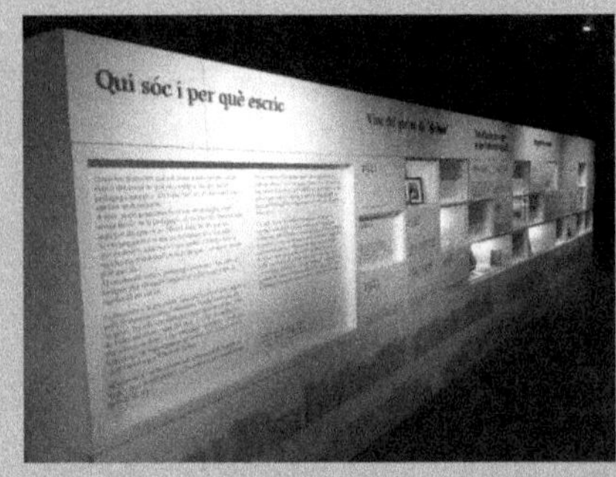

Opening hours: Monday to Saturday: 10–20h; Sundays and holidays: 10–14:30h
General information: 932 388 091 / 92 / 93
Tourist information: 012 in Catalonia
902 400 012 from outside Catalonia
www.gencat.cat/palaurobert

Bus: 7,16, 17, 22, 24, V17, 39
Metro: L3, L5 (Diagonal)
FGC: (railway) Provença-La Pedrera
Renfe: (railway) Passeig de Gràcia

the *Generalitat*. In 1997, the *Palau Robert* was inaugurated as one of the principal exhibition centres of the city. With this aim in mind, it has three adaptable spaces in which all kinds of temporary exhibitions, covering areas as diverse as photography, fashion, business or science, can be held. There is also an office of the Catalan tourism agency which acts as an information point for the city and the whole country. In addition, there is a concert hall and a bookshop. In 2003, the building's old garages were converted into two multipurpose spaces and in the magnificent gardens at the back the old wall, which ran along *Carrer Còrsega*, was replaced by a fence whose gate is open during the day to allow people to cross from the *Diagonal* to *Carrer Rosselló* under the shade of trees. A pleasant space that can be used for private functions all transformed into an open-air exhibition area and in which some of its nooks and crannies conceal interesting sculptures.

Avinguda Diagonal towards the River Llobregat

🏛 **The Fountain with the frog** (1912). This modernist fountain, inspired by nature, was the work of the sculptor Josep Campeny Santamaria. The bowl is made from stone and the bronze sculpture represents a boy with a frog in his hands; the frog acting as the fountain's spout.

🍴 **Farga.** Founded in 1957 by Jesús Farga, a master cake maker from Lleida, it is one of the most renowned bakeries and delicatessens in the city. This emblematic shop also has a cafeteria and restaurant which serves high-quality breakfast, lunch and dinners.

Rambla de Catalunya, 126

🏛 **Can Serra** (1903). The building in the foreground, *Can Serra*, is the work of modernist architect Josep Puig i Cadafalch, who designed the house to look like a Renaissance-inspired family mansion, though the corner tower, crowned by eaves in glazed ceramic tiles, has a rather medieval air. The sculptors Alfons Juyol i Bach and Eusebi Arnau created the medallions over the windows, which represents artists such as Wagner, Cervantes or the Catalan painter Marià Fortuny. The modern part of the building, in steel and glass, in the background and which frames the older building is the result of an expansion during the 1980s (designed by the architects Federico Correa and Alfons Milà) when the building was acquired by the *Diputació de Barcelona*, a body which coordinates the actions of various town and village councils in the province of Barcelona.

🏛 Church and convent of Pompeia (1910).

See the "Sagnier Route" section, pages 116-117.

🛍 Tous.

On the corner of *Diagonal* and the *Via Augusta*, this is a large modern shop (200 m² of open space opened in 2013). This jeweller's is an official agent for Rolex watches. They also make the now world famous teddy bear jewellery which they started in 1985. They have thirteen stores in Barcelona, forming part of their 400 sales points across the world. Since 1965, the couple, Salvador Tous and Rosa Oriol, natives of the city of Manresa, have been in charge of the business (a small jewellery repair workshop that Salvador's father had opened in 1920).

🛍 Unión Suiza.

Jewellery company from Barcelona founded in 1840 and currently managed by the sixth generation of the Vendrell family, has two distinct areas of activity. On the one hand, the sale of jewellery and watches from prestigious luxury brands in three of their own shops, two in Barcelona and one in Madrid, located in the nerve centres of these cities. On the other hand, the Unión Suiza de Distribución, dedicated to the distribution throughout Spain of the prestigious Kronos brand of watches, founded in 1930.

From Diagonal to Gran de Gràcia

Numbers 111-119

Deutsche Bank building. Designed in 1956-1959 as the head offices of the *Banco Comercial Transatlántico* by the architect Santiago Balcells (as stated on a small plaque on the façade), this 20 story building of 17,500 m², became the head office in Barcelona of the Deutsche Bank in 1994. Alterations to the building were carried out by the architects Francesc Albardaner and Josep Samsó, who devised its characteristic glass panels. In 2014, it changed hands again and an investment group converted it into a luxury hotel for the Four Seasons chain.

possible service. A personal assistant takes charge of all the staffing needs and can hire a chef, laundry facilities, a masseuse, a hairdresser, a personal shopper, a babysitter or book theatre tickets, among many more services.

 **Passeig de Gràcia 115 Apartments.** In 2004, after a refurbishment respecting the original façade due to its historic and artistic value (note the painted friezes) four floors of this building were opened as apartments for long or short stays in the city. Ever since 1901, it has always been in the hands of the Catalan industrialist family the Bertrands. Between 1980 and 2011, the ground floor was home to the double screen arthouse cinema the *Casablanca*.

Casa Bonaventura Ferrer (1906). The work of architect Pere Falqués i Urpí, it is popularly known as the *Palauet* (little palace). It is an excellent example of a modernist house, though more balanced and with fewer excesses than some of its neighbours. The façade consists of three vertical sections, the most notable feature of which is a bay on the main floor. The door and the balconies are of wrought iron and the crown of the building is of a baroque inspiration.

El Palauet Living Barcelona. Rooms in the mansion are rented out as six luxury suites with every

 **Parco.** One of the best Asian restaurants in the city. It claims to serve the best sushi. Minimalist decoration, diffuse lighting and a tranquil atmosphere.

Carrer Sèneca

This charming pedestrian street connecting with the *Via Augusta* is full of vintage furniture shops such as **Antique Boutique, Estudio Restauración** or **Ox Mobiliari.** They specialise in Scandinavian furniture from the 1950s or in handcrafted antique pieces. At number 13, there is the **Paulina Barcelona** boutique selling bags, handkerchiefs, purses and accessories, while at number 9-11, there is the **Miquel Alzueta** shopping gallery specialising in 20th Century furniture. In addition, there is a very good Catalan restaurant, the **Roig Robí**, at number 20, with a charming little interior garden.

Gran de Gràcia, 7

Casa Ramon Servent (1911). This work, by the modernist Catalan architect Emili Sala Cortés, is characterised by its polygonal bays on the first four floors and its floral ornamentation. The building is crowned by three added floors in a 19th Century style and four busts which, left to right, represent: Joan Fiveller (a 15th C. municipal councillor), Christopher Columbus (the discoverer of America), Miquel Servet (16th C. theologian and scientist) and Miguel de Cervantes (author of *Don Quixote)*, placed in chronological order.

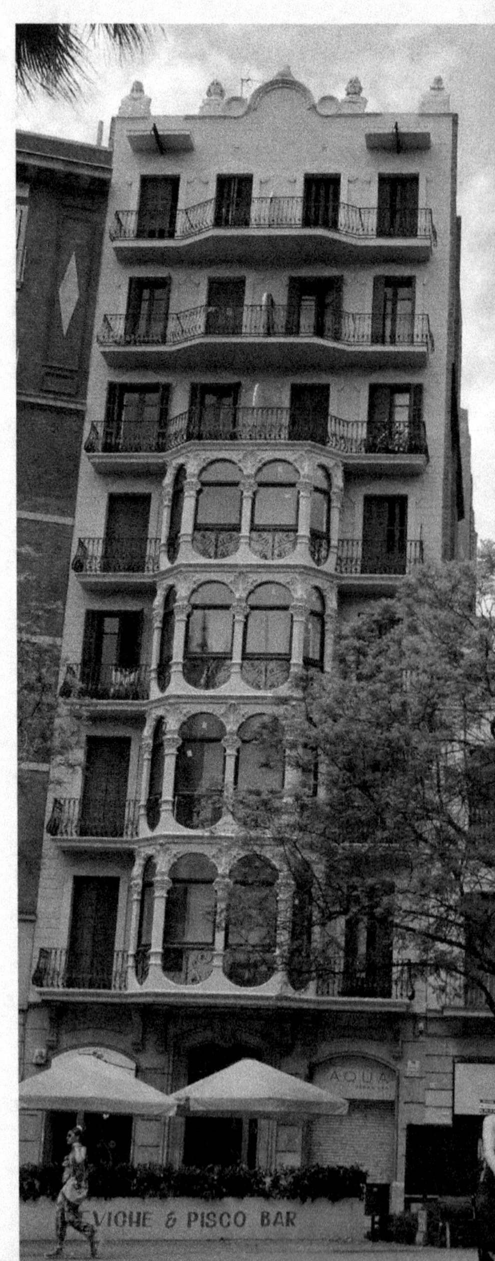

From Gran de Gràcia to Diagonal

Numbers 132-112

132

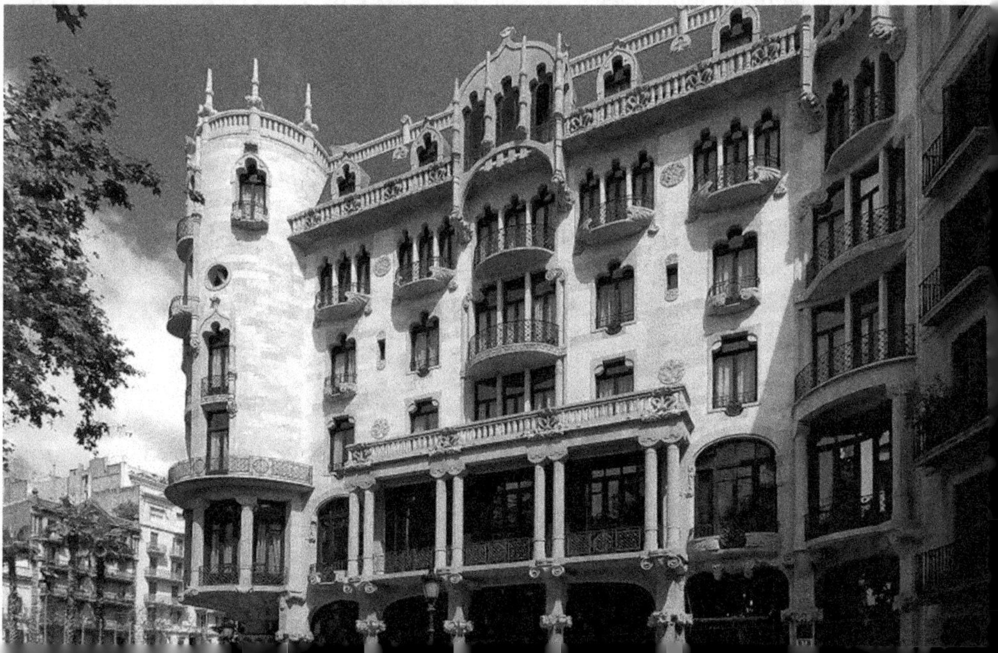

Casa Fuster (1911). This imposing modernist building, with a certain neo-Gothic air, rounds off the *Jardinets de Gràcia* and marks the beginning of *Carrer Gran de Gràcia*, the main commercial artery of the *Gràcia* district. It was the last work in Barcelona of the architect Lluís Domènech i Montaner. It was once the head offices of the *Enher* electric company, and today is the *Hotel Casa Fuster*. It was built on the site of the demolished *Juncosa* chocolate factory having been commissioned by the Mallorcan Mariano Fuster i Fuster, as a gift for his wife Consol Fabra i Puig, whose initials are marked in relief on the façade facing *Carrer Jesús*. Only the best materials were used in its construction: white marble on the façade, along with glass and slate contributing to its singular beauty. In its time it was the most expensive building in the city. On the corner there is a cylindrical tower with glass bays and sculptures reminiscent of swallows' nests.

Curious fact: On the façade is a plaque noting that the poet Salvador Espriu lived in this building from 1942 to 1972. Further up, at number 118, there is another, because the Catalan poet also lived there.

 **Casa Fuster** (5* Gran Luxe Monument). Crowning the *Eixample* is this hotel opened in 2004 which has become a meeting point for artists, intellectuals and travellers seeking a quiet and a unique place to stay or to do business in. The Blue View terrace, with its swimming pool, allows visitors to enjoy an aperitif or a light meal to the accompaniment of spectacular views of the *Passeig de Gràcia* and a good part of the city right down to the sea. The clientele, above all on summer evenings, oscillates between tourists and locals. It is a very pleasant place to chill out. *La Sala de Lectura* (reading room) on the ground floor, with its links to culture, attracts lead-

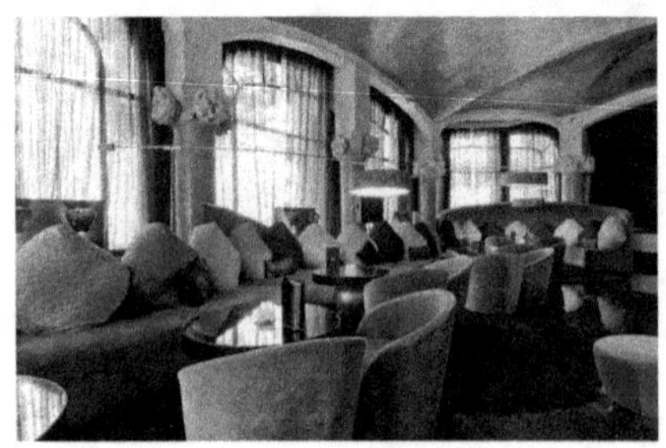

ing publishers and authors to the hotel. Additionally, a dozen conference halls are available where every type of event can be held. The first floor is home to the *Galaxó* restaurant, which offers Mediterranean and avant-garde cuisine. The *Cafè Vienès*, opened in the 1920s. Once the cultural epicentre of the city, it continues to be a unique meeting point and every Thursday evening is transformed into the *Club de Jazz*.

130

 **Blu Barcelona.** Marc Codina's jewellery store, where the stars are diamonds, sapphires, emeralds and rubies.

128

Suites Center Barcelona. Fifteen deluxe suites with everything necessary to enjoy a stay in the city.

Kiton. The Italian brand Kiton, specialises in high fashion and accessories for both men and women. It has 54 branches, like this one, spread across countries such as France, Russia, Ukraine, the USA, China or the United Arab Emirates.

🍴 **Ottavia.** Ice cream makers originally from the island of Madeira offering tropical flavoured ices in a very original wrapping.

🛍 **Lupo.** This brand, which started in 1920 in a workshop in the *Gràcia* district, opened this boutique in 2014, in addition to the one it had already had in *Carrer Mallorca.* They specialise in luxury bags.

Curious fact: Until 2013, the ground floor that Lupo now occupies had been the *Roquer* bookshop, specialising in art books and children's books.

🛍 **L'Òptica Universitària.** This is one of 46 opticians in a chain that was founded on the university campus on the *Diagonal* in Barcelona. Thanks to irresistible prices, an intelligent policy of discounts and an impeccable service they have gained the confidence of many young people (and some not so young) when it comes to choosing spectacles or sunglasses.

Carrer Bonavista

This street owes its name to the wonderful views over the *Passeig de Gràcia* that its buildings on the mountain side have. On that same side there are some modernist façades with sgrafitti, such as numbers 5, 7 or 11.

Jardinets de Gràcia

The part of *Passeig de Gràcia* above the *Diagonal* has been officially known as the *Jardins de Salvador Espriu* since 1991, in honour of the Catalan poet, who lived in the *Casa Fuster*. However, the people of Barcelona usually refer to it as the *Jardinets de Gràcia*. The gardens were constructed, in 1929, as part of the International Exposition of Barcelona, under the guidance of garden designer Nicolau Rubió i Tudurí. Their role was to act as a link between the *Passeig* and the *Gràcia* district, an ancient town that had been annexed by the city in 1897.

A trio of sculptures

The *Obelisc* or the *Llapis*. Located in the centre of the *Plaça de Joan Carles I*, this sculpture dates back to 1936, when it was designed in honour of Francesc Pi i Margall (the President of the first Spanish Republic in 1873). It was the work of Adolf Florensa and Josep Vilaseca. Over time, it acquired its popular nickname the *Llapis,* because of its resemblance to a pencil. Today, it stands alone, but until 2011, it was accompanied by a statue represent-

ing the victory of Franco's troops at the end of the Spanish Civil War. This statue had replaced an earlier figure of a nude woman, placed on top of the obelisk (which represented the Republic) that had been the work of sculptor Josep Viladomat. The square had once had another popular name: the *Cinc d'Oros*, because in 1909, four elements with a round base surrounding a central circle had been placed there. Seen from above, these looked like the equivalent of the five of diamonds in the Spanish card deck, which consists of five golden coins.

🏛 *Solc.* As part of the celebrations of the centenary of the birth of the poet Salvador Espriu, in 2013, the sculptor Frederic Amat was commissioned to create a sculpture for the garden the poet would have seen when looking out the window of *Casa Fuster*. The result is a horizontal cement trench that appears to be in dialogue with the "Pencil" and which has a funereal air, very close in spirit to the world of Espriu.

🏛 **Hommage of Pompeu Fabra and** *La lectura.* At the upper end of this gardened area is a plaque upon which metal letters state *"Barcelona a Pompeu Fabra"*, in homage to the linguist who defined the standard Catalan language and drew up its first dictionary. Close by, is a relief sculpture representing a woman reading. This dates from 1948 and is the work of Josep Clarà. A little further up, there are two fountains: the one is a small drinking fountain, while in the centre there is a larger decorative fountain.

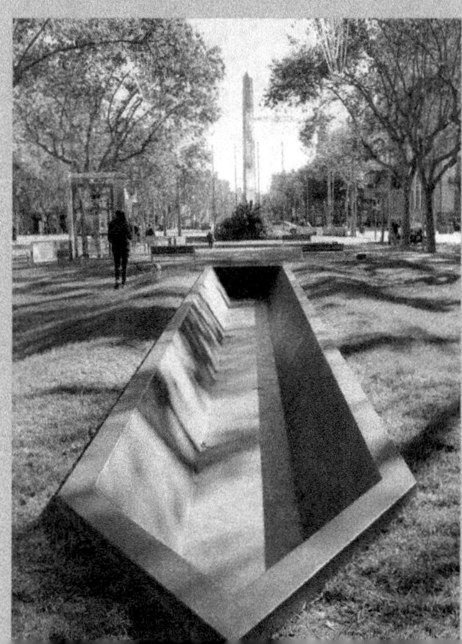

🛍 **BOO.** A fashion boutique for men and women, one of the temples of ultra-modernity among the hipster set in the city. The decoration is exquisite and it is even possible to try clothes on within a Barcelona telephone booth from the 1920s.

120

🍴 **Buenas Migas.** At the foot of an impressive neoclassic building you can eat home-made pasta and breads, along with other traditional recipes from Liguria (Italy) and Cornwall (UK) the two places where Clare and Patrick (the founders of this successful chain of Barcelonan *focacceries*) are from.

116

🍴 **L'Eggs.** This restaurant is run by Paco Pérez, who trained with chefs such as Ferran Adrià or Joan Roca. The original touch here is to make eggs the centre of the chef's creations. His intention is "to do something different, something fun that everyone will enjoy; something for everyone that is affordable". Poached eggs, fried eggs, boiled eggs, eggs with eels and every type of omelette. There are also dishes without eggs and it has an outdoor terrace.

🏢 **Casa Gràcia Barcelona Hostel.** This modernist building is home to a hostel for travellers who wish to be right in the centre of Barcelona. It has rooms for from 2 to 6 people, common rooms, such as a kitchen, living room, dining room or terrace and also a luxury suite.

Casa Lluís Ferrer-Vidal (1916). A residential building designed by Eduard Ferrés i Puig on a plot on which one of the five single family chalets belonging to the Marquis of Salamanca had stood. They had been built in 1865 by Elies Rogent. The current building had two stories added to it, which necessitated removal of the dome which used to crown it. Each floor received a different treatment, though the semicircular bay with its arches and stained glass on the first floor (which supports the open balcony on the floor above) obviously stands out. The coat of arms over the main door has the initials of its first owner the industrialist and politician.

Galeria Comas. An art gallery that is open to the public. It is possible to go up to the first floor of the building and admire collections by local painters (changed every 3 weeks), as well as some stained glass that was inspired by Goya and which decorates the patio. The gallery has been around since 1979.

F. Roca. This jeweller's, specialising in diamonds, has been offering a purchasing service to the public, along with a diamond cutting service, they also have their own designers and workshops.

 **Tween.** This clothes chain, originally from Turkey, has been dressing men all over the world for 20 years via its more than 150 boutiques.

112

Casa Garriga (1911). Another example of the work of the architect Enric Sagnier i Villavecchia, this house on the corner with *Carrer Còrsega*, has a notable stone façade, especially the part facing *Passeig de Gràcia*, where the type of stone used and the windows are different. It was commissioned by the financier Rupert Garriga i Miranda and in order to construct it one of the five chalets that the Marquis of Salamanca had had built in 1865, between Carrers Còrsega and Bonavista had to be demolished. The two upper stories were added in the 1930s, but unlike in many other cases, these harmonised with the building.

Diagonal towards the Besòs

△

Diagonal, 442

🏛 **Casa Comalat** (1911). A modernist building, the work of architect Salvador Valeri i Pupurull, characterised by its two magnificent façades which echo the *Casa Batlló* by Antoni Gaudí with its sculpted stone balconies, wrought iron railings, curves and abundant floral ornamentation. Of particular note are the main door and the balconies on the first floor which form a central gallery run-

ning between the first and second floors and the giant harlequin's hat crowning the building. The building also has another, more colourful, façade at 316 *Carrer Còrsega*, observe the irregular bays and polychromatic wooden galleries with their venetian blinds as well as the ceramics and stained glass.

Diagonal, 416-420

🏛 **Casa Terrades** (1905). Continuing along *Avinguda Diagonal*, some meters away, stands a building that, for obvious reasons, is known as the *Casa de les Punxes* (spiky house). This singular building was designed

by the architect Josep Puig i Cadafalch in 1905 as a commission from the Terrades brothers, who wanted to join together three buildings they owned. The building has a clear mediaeval aspect, characteristic of European Gothic and is crowned by six towers finished off with conical spires. The most characteristic elements on the façade are the brickwork, the decorative stone panels covering it and, in particular, the floral patterns on the bays, along with the modernist balconies, the double sloping roofs and a representation of St George with the legend: "Patron saint of Catalonia, give us back our liberty".

This building was declared to be a Historical national monument in 1975 and Site of Cultural Interest in 1976.

Diagonal, 383

Silbon. A boutique belonging to a firm from Cordoba which sells a wide range of male fashion, footwear and an assortment of accessories in a very British style. Comfort in consonance with elegance.

Diagonal, 373

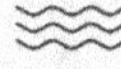 **Palau Baró de Quadras** (1904). This spectacular modernist building stands on the *Avinguda Diagonal* and also at number 279 *Carrer Rosselló*. It is one of

the most singular gems in Barcelona's architectural heritage. On the one hand, it is a neo-Gothic palace; on the other, pure modernism. In 1900, the rich industrialist the Baró de Quadras commissioned the architect Josep Puig i Cadafalch to refurbish this block of flats. Seen from the *Diagonal*, the sculptures of mediaeval and renaissance characters, the flowers, the coat of arms and the long gallery transport us directly to Gothic palaces in the north of Europe. From *Carrer Rosselló*, in contrast, we can admire the remains of the old building and an example of a more conventional modernism with carved floral elements. In the interior, there are the familiar and quite diverse elements associated with the work of Puig i Cadafalch:

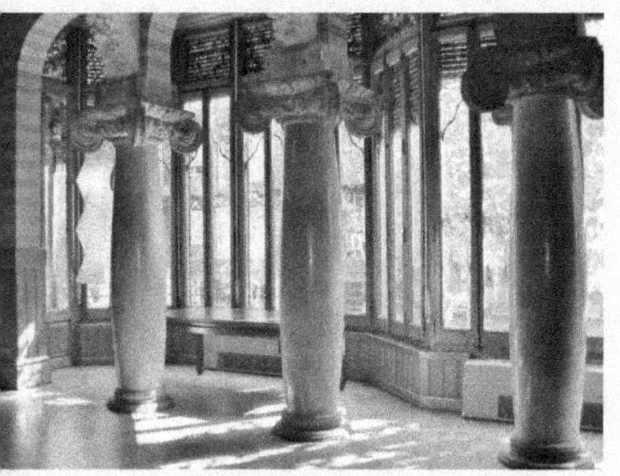

colourful ceramics influenced by Islam, Gothic-like sculptural elements and a spectacular stairway in carved stone leading up to the first floor. The building was declared a national heritage site in 1976 and today is the head offices of the internationally known Catalan cultural organisation the *Institut Ramon Llull*.

From Diagonal to Rosselló

Numbers 110–104

Carmina Shoemaker. This, now international, firm was founded in 1997. However, its origins date back to 1866 when Matias Pujadas opened a small made-to-measure shoemakers in the town of Inca (Mallorca). Their shoes, for men and women, are characterised by the traditional double Goodyear stitching, which offers durability, flexibility, comfort and waterproofing.

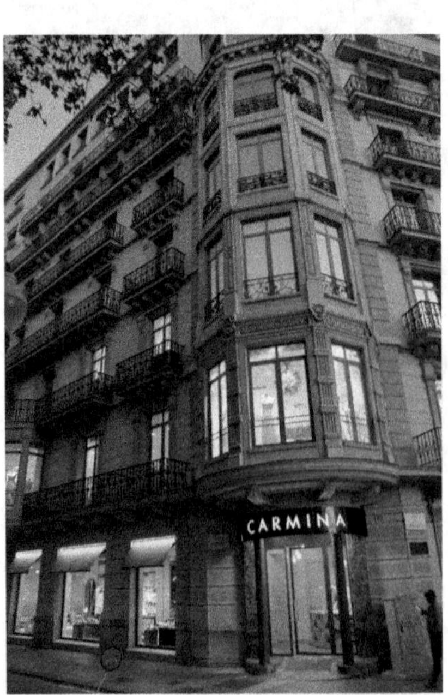

Gratacós. Craftsmanship, research, beauty and creativity. These have been the foundations of this fabric store since 1940. Despite the arrival of luxury and multinational brands, it has maintained its essence and presence for all these years. It was founded by Antonio Gratacós and Josefina Ortiz de la Orden and since then has dressed famous personalities such as Michelle Obama, Mònica Naranjo, Céline Dion or the Spanish and Dutch Royal Families. Its shop window creations are famous, as are the examples of all their fabrics on vertical display in the interior along with the fine woodwork which combines with contemporary coloured elements.

🏛 **Casa Jacint Esteva** (1939). This building was designed by the architect Pere Benavent de Barberà. It has a very different aesthetic from the rest of the Boulevard with a more rationalist air and a rather austere façade in tones of beige. It is an example from the Modern Movement which dominated architecture from the second decade of the 20ᵗʰ Century.

🏛 **Fundació Frederic Mompou.** This foundation is dedicated to conserving, and promoting the studio of the magnificent Catalan composer Frederic Mompou (1893-1987). Located on the first floor, where the composer lived, it was opened in 2006 by his wife and heir, Carme Bravo. Mompou is best known for his delicate, intimate and miniaturist pieces for piano.

🛍 **Valentino.** A historic firm that has dressed celebrities such as Audrey Hepburn, Jacqueline Onassis or Elisabeth Taylor. Present in 90 countries, it has 160 boutiques and more than 1,300 sales points. Valentino has stated that his "Valentino Vermilion" was directly inspired by Barcelona. To be exact, by an incredibly red dress he saw one night at the *Gran Teatre del Liceu* opera house.

FreyWille. A Viennese jeweller's, with more than 100 shops in 35 countries. They specialise in enamelled jewellery decorated in floral or geometric patterns that are always artistic and striking.

TCN. These three letters are the initials of the Catalan designer Toton Comella Noé. He burst onto the scene in 1984 with a collection of swimwear in Lycra and cotton, a combination not seen before. His swimwear, like his underwear and lingerie, is characterised by its comfort, glamour, sensuality and simplicity.

Jofré. This boutique, founded in Reus in 1929, has five sales points across Barcelona. With an amiable, minimalist decoration, it sells the most famous brands in luxury clothing such as Yves Saint Laurent, Chloé or Earl Jeans.

Wolford. This Austrian company specialises in lingerie for women. Founded in 1949, they created their Luxor line of nylons in 1975 (the first street proof tights). They also introduced spandex and silky feel underwear, as well as the first bodysuits in the 1980s. Since 2000, they have allied with some great fashion designers to offer all kinds of clothes for women.

Carrer Rosselló towards the River Besòs

Rosselló 265

Omm (5*). A comfortable and luxurious hotel of a fun, modern design. It has 91 rooms, a spa, swimming pool, terraces and above all the **Roca Moo** restaurant (with a Michelin star),

advised by the *Celler de Can Roca* and run by the chef Juan Pretel. The more informal **Roca Bar** restaurant is an ideal spot for sandwiches, tapas and the chef's recommendation for that day.

Rosselló, 271

La Inmaculada Concepción. A furniture and decoration shop specialising in vintage or retro material. Of special note are their recycled objects and custom furniture.

Rosselló, 275

Dos i una. Here you can find a wide variety of accessories and games, both for children and adults; everything from a 1980s t-shirt through old postcards to analogue cameras, flower-shaped tea cups, chrome cuckoo clocks, and board games that our parents and grandparents played. A must visit place for time travellers and lovers of colourful gadgets.

Rosselló, 240

Casa Josep Arús (1889). This is one of the few remaining examples of a neoclassical single family mansion on the *Eixample*, with a gallery on the first floor and two higher lateral sections. It was designed by Antoni Serra Pujals.

Rosselló, 238

Actual (3*). A tastefully decorated hotel with rooms for individuals or for families of up to six. Combines the charm of a boutique hotel with the services of a grand hotel.

From Rosselló to Provença

Numbers 102–92

 **Stella McCartney.** Opened in 2012, the striking colourful decoration in the shop window prepares you for the style of the *prêt-à-porter* range of this British designer, the daughter of Beatle Paul McCartney. She uses no leather in her designs.

Paseo de Gracia (1*). The slogan of this downtown one star hotel is: "Sleep cheap in a zone that's chic!". Large comfortable well-lit rooms for families at a reasonable price.

Yves Saint Laurent. YSL was the first fashion house to introduce the concept of luxury *prêt-à-porter* with their *Rive Gauche* collection in 1996. It was also the first to reincorporate the tuxedo and its traditionally masculine offerings, such as the suit, into their line for women. A select and delicately plush boutique.

 **Michael Kors.** The most curious thing about this firm, one of the most important design outfits in the United States, is that they arrived in Catalonia in 2010 with a store at the *Roca del Vallès* outlet mall. Their aim is to "Combine American comfort with European luxury". That same year they also opened this store on *Passeig de Gràcia* in 200 m^2 of space where you can find their cheerful, easily combin-

able pieces such as watches, shoes, jewellery and perfumes.

🛍 **Iranzo.** This is a hairdresser's and beauty and image assessment parlour offering individualised treatment since 1924. Some of their most famous clientele have been King Juan Carlos I, Gabriel Garcia Márquez, Joan Manuel Serrat, Joan Brossa, Johan Cruyff, Alfredo Krauss and Maradona. Of course, hundreds more heads have been under their scissors or experienced their renowned wet razor cuts.

🛍 **Camper.** This is the oldest company in the shoe sector in Spain. Freedom, comfort and creativity are the key words that the Mallorcan Lorenzo Fluixà has wanted to associate with his brand since 1975. In his modern, no-nonsense, but very innovative boutiques can be found footwear for men, women and children. They have another shop at number 2.

🛍 **Salvatore Ferragamo.** Known as the "shoemaker to the stars" he emigrated from his native Italy to California when he was still very young and did not return until he had triumphed, providing shoes for half of the Hollywood universe: Audrey Hepburn, Judy Garland, Marilyn Monroe, Greta Garbo, Brigitte Bardot, Madonna or Nicole Kidman to name but a few.

🏛 **Fundació Suñol.** This private non-profit foundation established in 2002 is aimed at "promoting, supporting and disseminating art in general and that of our own collection, as well as conserving Suñol's art and studio. We provide grants for artists, students and researchers, promoting Catalan art throughout the world".

Opening hours: Monday to Friday: 11–14h and 16–20h. Saturdays: 16–20h. Sundays and holidays, closed. It is possible to arrange other times

Prices: General ticket: 4 € / Reduced ticket: 2 €

Information: 934 961 032
www.fundaciosunol.org

Autobús: 6, 7, 15, 16, 17, 20, 22, 24, 28, 33, 34, 39, 43, 44, 45, 47. Bus Turístic, north and south routes
Metro: L3, L5 (Diagonal)
FGC: (railway) Provença-La Pedrera
Renfe: (railway) Passeig de Gràcia

The courtyard of tthe Fundació Suñol

In addition to programming mono-graphic and avant-garde exhibitions, they have more than 1000 m² of exhibition space displaying more than 1,200 works by artists such as: Warhol, Picasso, Miró, Dalí, Tàpies, Man Ray, Gargallo, Giacometti, Gordillo, Zush, Boetti, Solano, Lootz, Navarro or Plensa, among others.

 **Bottega Veneta.** An Italian brand specialising in leather goods. They have 150 m² of deluxe exclusivity in a convivial interior thanks to walnut tables, earthy tones and carefully chosen details in leather and steel. This is the only shop in Spain where you can find the firm's collections.

96

Casa Casas-Carbó (1894). This modernist building is in the catalogue of the city's architectural heritage. It was designed by the architect Antoni Rovira i Rabassa and belonged to the famous

modernist painter Ramon Casas, who lived on the first floor and often welcomed his great friend the artist Santiago Rusiñol; as is evidenced on two plaques at different heights on the façade. Of particular note are the stonework on the balconies, the main entrance and the building's crown with the same floral decoration repeated on a line of small windows. Also of note is the front door with its two wooden panels decorated in wrought iron.

Vinçon. The origins of this establishment go back to 1941, when Enrique Levi (a Jew), Hugo Vinçon (a German) and the Amat brothers inaugurated *"Regalos Hugo Vinçon"*.

However, it was not until 1967, and later in 1973, with the opening of the exhibition hall for industrial and graphic work, that it really took off. Artists, architects and designers from all over the world began to exhibit here and the place became an indispensable meeting point for lovers of objects associated with design and decoration. The two floors of the establishment are treated as if it were all one huge exhibition, in perfect harmony with the majesty of the building.

Not to be missed: From the patio of the building you can see the rear façade of *La Pedrera*.

🏛 **Casa Codina** (1898). A modernist building by the architect Antoni Rovira i Rabassa. The most striking aspect is the gallery taking up the first floor which dominates the stone façade; but also note, higher up, the windows of different heights with a central balcony and the wrought iron work on the railings of the rooftop terrace.

🏛 **Casa Milà or La Pedrera** (1912). See the "Of particular note" section, pages 104-105.

🛍 **Casa Viva.** Articles for the home and decoration: everything for the dining room, kitchen and bathroom along with small items of furniture for both the interior and exterior. Also travel articles and a wide range of books on topics related to Barcelona.

Casa Milà or *La Pedrera*

This is the jewel in the crown of the *Passeig de Gràcia*. Popularly known as *La Pedrera* because of its purported resemblance to an open quarry, this modernist building, the work of Antoni Gaudí, was built between 1906 and 1912. It was commissioned by the married couple Pere Milà Camps and Roser Segimon Artells. It was declared a world Heritage site by Unesco in 1984. Apart from the wrought iron work on its balconies and the undulating, almost animated, shapes of its façade, inspired by organic forms in nature, its principal characteristic (also perhaps the least known aspect of this architectural gem) is that the only structural walls in the building are those of the staircase. It was Antoni Gaudí's last private work before he dedicated the rest of his life to working on his *Sagrada Família* cathedral. Despite the numerous obstacles faced when building it, Gaudí managed to ensure it was not subject to municipal building regulations due to its great artistic and monumental significance. During the Spanish Civil War it was occupied by the PSUC (Unified Socialist Party of Catalonia); in 1946, Milà's widow sold the building to a property firm who built thirteen apartments in the attic. From 1966, it hosted offices, a bingo hall, a private school and a hostel. Today it is one of the most visited attractions in the city, with more than a million visitors annually.

In 1986, the bank *Caixa de Catalunya* acquired the building and made it the flagship of its foundation. Today, the *Fundació Catalunya-La Pedrera* has transformed the space into a first rate cultural centre which regularly holds important exhibitions, conferences cycles, poetry recitals, concerts and audiovisual projections in the magnificent auditorium on the ground floor

Opening hours: Monday to Sunday: 9–20h. From 3rd of November: 9–18:30h. Closed: 25th of December. 1st of January: 11–18:30h

Prices: Adult: 20,50€ / Student card: 16,50€ / Disabled guests: 16,50€ / Minors (-6): free; (-12): 10,25€

Reservations: in advance to groups for more than 10 people: grups@lapedrera.com

Information: 902 202 138, www.lapedrera.com. Access for disabled guests

Bus: 7,16, 17, 22, 24, V17, 39
Metro: L3, L5 (Diagonal
FGC: (railway) Provença-La Pedrera
Renfe: (railway) Passeig de Gràcia

of the building or on the rooftop terrace on summer nights. It is especially recommendable to visit *La Pedrera* at night (possible all year) and discover its secrets through projections, holograms and all kinds of sensory effects accompanied by a delightful evening meal or a glass of champagne.
You must not miss:

The terrace: an unusual and extremely artistic rooftop whose ventilation towers and chimneys easily transport the visitors to other worlds or other eras.
The Espai Gaudí: the attic of the building which previously housed washrooms and clothes drying lines and which today offers the visitor explanations and glimpses of the creations and visions of this Catalan architectural genius beneath 270 catenary arches in flat brickwork.
The apartment: this can be found on the fourth floor. It offers a vision of how a bourgeois Catalan family of the 19th Century lived. Visitors can view everything from the furniture or appliances of the epoch to the interior distribution and decorative elements of the period.

The patios: a real spectacle of light, structures and colours in which organic forms, mural paintings and the most pure modernism are placed at the service of architecture.

The exhibition hall: located on the first floor, this was the residence of the Milà family. Of particular note is the staircase in the vestibule with its wrought iron banisters, mural paintings sculpted stone columns and Gaudí's characteristic *trencadís* (broken ceramic tile mosaics).

From Provença to Mallorca

Numbers 88–82

88

**Prada.** This firm now has a network of 461 shops throughout the world shared out among their main brands: Prada, MiuMiu, Church and Car Shoe. The company, led by Miuccia Prada and Patrizio Bertelli opened this enormous boutique in 2013. Here, immersed in the black and gold of the brand, you can find all of their *prêt-à-porter* collections for men and women as well as exclusive luxury items in leather, accessories, perfumes and footwear.

86

**Longchamp.** They started in 1948, in Paris, manufacturing leather items for smokers. Before long, they were one of the most appreciated brands of bags and every

type of leather goods. This shop has 700 m² on two floors. Among many other articles, you can acquire the emblem of the brand which so many celebrities and top-models have sported, season after season, for the last 20 years: the bag known as *Le pliage*.

Curious fact: This building was once the headquarters of the insurance company *Sociedad de Seguros Mutuos Contra Incendios* and on the façade you can still see the original reliefs representing a family watching a house go up in flames.

84

Royal Passeig de Gràcia (4*). This hotel, with all the usual comforts associated with an establishment of this category, has one of the most spectacular terraces in the city, the 83.3 Terrace, with 300° views. The curious name refers to the size of the 83.3 cm modules used in constructing the building. Once the head offices of the now vanished *Banca Catalana*, it was designed by the architects Enric Tous and Josep M. Fargas Falp and constructed between 1965 and 1968. The Royal Hotel chain decided to keep the original façade and the original structural components, made up of a modular structure in which glass panels alternate with parabolic insulating surfaces. The hotel has 124 totally sound-proofed rooms. Of particular note

is the interior patio and the Garden and Warren spaces, the latter between the ground floor and the first floor, where you can now see the famous Warren beams, which were hidden for many years.

 **BBVA.** The ground floor of the building houses the main office in Barcelona of this successful bank.

82

 Cartier. Walking into this boutique, on the ground floor of an elegant marble and glass building constructed in the year 2000, it is easy to see why, since the beginning of the last century, the leading lights of society have fallen at Cartier's feet. Cartier represents luxury and refinement taken to its ultimate extreme. The salons in this 450 m² boutique are lined with white oak. There are three majestic vertical display cabinets where you can discover, admire, and who knows, even acquire jewellery, watches, accessories and perfumes from this exclusive firm.

 Suárez. This company has its origins in the Basque country. It was founded, in 1943, by Emiliano Suárez Faffián. Since then the family business has grown thanks to the eminence of its clientele, the quality of its own collections and the top brands it represents. Situated on the corner of *Carrer Mallorca*, the boutique has a 34 m long shop window and an elegant interior space of 800 m².

From Mallorca to València

Casa Julià (1874). On the other corner of *Carrer Mallorca* stands this work by the prestigious Valencian architect Rafael Guastavino i Moreno. All that remains of the original building is the neo-Greek façade, since the interior was completely demolished some years back. Although not well known in Spain because he emigrated to the United States, Guastavino was considered by Lluís Domènech i Montaner to be an architect of exceptional talent. He was a key figure in US architecture at the end of the 19th Century, thanks to his construction of great cement and brick vaults patented in the US as the Guastavino System.

🛍 **Louis Vuitton.** Inaugurated with great solemnity in September 2013, this is a huge, open, light-filled space. Here we can find, at not exactly modest prices, everything from ready-to-wear items through luxury goods for travel to the brand's flagship collections of leather work.

78

🛍 **Chopard.** A Swiss jeweller's founded by Louis-Ulysse Chopard in 1860. Since then it has become a benchmark for innovation in deluxe jewellery and watch making. High-quality accessories are also available here.

🛍 **Twenty One.** A hairdressers and beauty parlour where Esther Llongueras, the daughter of hairdresser Lluís Llongueras, and her ample team of professionals offer clients a top-quality, totally personalised treatment.

🍴 **Pomarada.** A restaurant and bar occupying more than 800 m². They specialise in Asturian cuisine (bean dishes, cider, rice pudding) and pizzas as well as creative and avant-garde Mediterranean cooking. The restaurant has a concierge, a lift, a terrace, both à la carte and set menus and rooms big enough to seat all kinds of groups; all around their pleasant interior patio.

🍴 **La Vinoteca Torres.** A restaurant specialising in wines. Together with the Sagardi group, they offer a unique culinary and oenological experience, thanks to a wide range of wines from the Torres group.

76

🛍 **Gucci.** Smoked mirrors, polished gold, glass, marble and Rosewood is what we find when we walk into this luxurious 400 m² world, inaugurated in 2012. This Italian brand, founded in 1921 by Guccio Gucci in a modest workshop in Florence, now has its world-famous and omnipresent logotype on all kinds of fashion articles, suitcases, watches, shoes or perfumes. And for a little more, you can also have your bag embossed with your initials in gold.

74

🏛 **Casa Coma** (1907). This work by the prolific architect Enric Sagnier i Villavecchia, is notable for its sinuous profiles both on its stone balconies and its gallery, as well as on the cornice which crowns the façade. The central gallery, in stone with floral motifs, is framed by some slender columns and crowned by a balcony, which is a terrace for the upper floor. It has a spectacular marble entranceway, watched over by four Corinthian columns.

👜 **Bvlgari.** A leading Italian jeweller's, based in Rome since 1884, that adds glamour and transcendence to its original creations in jewellery, watches, leather work, accessories and perfumes . You can even stay in its exclusive hotels and resorts.

Chanel. More than just #5. It is not only about Coco the seamstress, the hat shop on the Parisian Boulevard of Malesherbes, opened in 1909, or the tanned bodies within simple straight comfortable lines that revolutionised fashion at the beginning of the 20th Century. Today the name evokes luxury and prestige through its 170 boutiques all over the world. This 190 m² establishment has various modern shop windows where you can admire products and designs created by the great high fashion genius Karl Lagerfeld. Beyond fashion and perfumes, Chanel offers jewellery, watches, accessories, make up and treatments.

Majestic Hotel & Spa (1918) (5* *grand luxe*). Initially it was called the *Majestic Inglaterra*, but in 1940 it dropped the "England" to become simply the Majestic. Today, the Majestic has more than 270 rooms and suites with all of the comforts you would expect from a luxury establishment in a neoclassical style building. The hotel's restaurant has as its culinary consultant Nandu Jubany, a point of reference in haute cuisine and garlanded with a Michelin star. We would especially recommend the spa, which has steam rooms and a sauna and offers several different body treatments. Another recommendation is *La Dolce Vitae*, on the top of the building; this is a terrace around a swimming pool from which you can contemplate a magnificent panorama of the city.

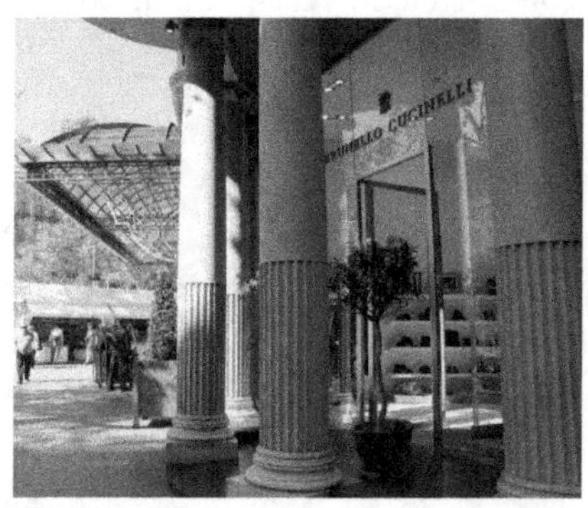

Curious fact: The Majestic becomes the campaign headquarters for the *Convergència i Unió* political coalition during elections. It was here that the famous "Majestic Pact" was drawn up on the 28th April 1996, in which the Catalan coalition promised to support the Spanish right wing *Partit Popular* in return for certain compensations. Among the many famous people who have stayed here are Queen Maria Cristina, Antonio Machado, Joan Miró, Charles Trenet or Federico Garcia Lorca.

Brunello Cuccinelly. This deluxe Italian firm specialising in high fashion for men and women can be found on the ground floor of the Hotel Majestic and also has an entrance in *Carrer València*. The interior is designed to invite you to relax thanks to its earthy tones, its ivory and the family photographs which hark back to the Italian childhood of the founder and the craft tradition of the company.

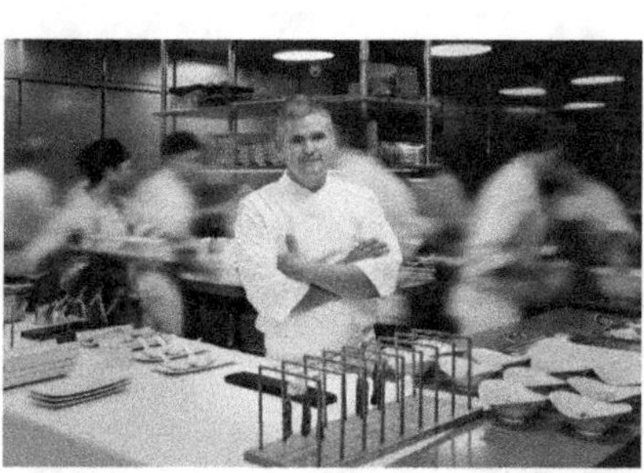

Carrer València towards the River Besòs

València, 267

🍴 **Nueve Reinas.** An Argentinean restaurant for lovers of fine meats, gnocchi and even gizzard. A piece of Argentina in Barcelona.

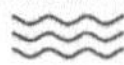

València, 274

🛍 **Top Natural Fibers.** Clothes made from cashmere, silk, linen or any other natural fibre, either unadorned or with stamped patterns.

València, 284

🏛 **Museu Egipci.** The *Fundació Arqueològica Clos - Museu Egipci de Barcelona* not only has one of the most important private collections of Egyptian art and culture in Europe, it is also an organisation committed to researching, studying and publicizing the ancient civilisation of the Pharaohs. Having more than 2000 m² of space and more than 1000 pieces, ranging from sarcophagi through mummies to jewels and amulets, there is also the possibility of a guided tour by expert Egyptologists. In addition to the permanent and temporary exhibitions, the museum also offers nocturnal visits, with dramatised scenes, as well as a visit centred on Egyptian culinary arts in which visitors can taste products that formed part of that ancient civilisation's diet.

The Egyptian Museum was created in 1992 when Jordi Clos Llombart, a Catalan businessmen, patron of culture and President of the hotel chain Derby Hotels, presented part of his private collection to the *Hotel Claris*. This involved a selection of 70 pieces from a collection which he had begun in 1975. Soon after, its success was such that it

led to the creation of the Clos Archaeological Foundation and only two years later to the opening of Barcelona's Egyptian Museum on the *Rambla de Catalunya*; which became the first monographic museum dedicated to the topic in Spain. In the year 2000, it moved to its present location and, since then, has received more than two million visitors.

Winter opening hours (7/01–21/06 and of 12/09–30/11): Monday to Saturday: 10–14h and 16–20h; Sunday: 10–14h. Christmas (1/12– 5/01): Monday to Saturday: 10–20h; Sunday: 10–14h

Summer opening hours (22/06– 11/09): Monday to Saturday: 10–20h; Sunday: 10–14h

Easter and holidays: Monday to Saturday: 10–20h; Sunday: 10–14h

Closed 1st and 6th of January, 25th and 26th of December. Guided tours free: Saturday 11h (Catalan) and 17h (Spanish), included on the entrance. Visits for groups, booking the tour previously visites@museuegipci.com

Prices: General ticket: 11 € / Reduced ticket: 8 € (students, unemployeds, large families and single-parents, young card, teaching ticket, over 65 years old and minors among 5 and 15 years) / Free ticket minors of 5 years old and members of: Egyptian Museum Friends Club of Barcelona, Super 3 Club, ICOM, guests of Derby Hotels

Information: 934 880 188
www.museuegipci.com

Bus: 7, 16, 17, 20, 22, 24, 28, 39, 45, H10. Bus Turístic, north and south routes

Metro: L1 (Catalunya), L2 (Passeig de Gràcia), L3 (Catalunya, Passeig de Gràcia), L4 (Passeig de Gràcia)

FGC: (railway) Provença-La Pedrera

Renfe: (railway) Passeig de Gràcia

València, 286

Les gens que j'aime. One the most curious named bars in the city ("The people I love"). Its origins go back to Barcelona's *"gauche divine"* in the 1960s. Modernist in aesthetic, dimly lit, with antique objects and furniture and lots of red velvet, the place invites you to converse in private, while listening to soul music.
Open from 18:30 to 2:00.

The Sagnier Route

Enric Sagnier i Villavecchia (Barcelona, 1858-1931) is perhaps the architect who designed the most buildings in the city of Barcelona, almost three hundred are credited to him. He was a member of the Catholic Association of Artists of the Circle of St Luke and his Modernism is more Neo-Gothic while his classicism demonstrates more French influences. This route, which begins at the southernmost point of *Plaça Catalunya* and ends at the top of *Passeig de Gràcia* focuses on five very different buildings: a bank, two residential buildings, a school and a church, all carried out with elegance and a little eccentricity.

▎Plaça Catalunya, 2
The former Banca Arnús (1927). Situated on the corner of *Plaça Catalunya* and *La Rambla* and based on a building from 1873 to which was added an adjacent building, the owners came up with the idea of giving the resulting joint building more architectural weight. Using the French influenced classicism that Sagnier was cultivating at the time, the architect resolved the union between the existing building and the addition of a new floor by harmonising them thanks to the domes on either side and those used for the new main entrance. The building was initially the *Banca Arnús*, then later the *Banco Central*. It became famous in May 1981 when an armed bank robbery there turned into a siege with many hostages that lasted over thirty hours. The situation caused a great deal of tension in the city and across the whole country.

▎Passeig de Gràcia, 2
Casa Pons (1884). See pages 141-142.

▎Diputació, 250
Casa Rupert Garriga Nogués (1901). From the outside, this building gives the impression of being a palace belonging to a single family. The balcony over the main entrance is sustained by four huge sculpted corbels with a theme symbolising different stages of our lives; the work of Eusebi Arnau. One unusual feature is the annex on the ground and first floors which reveals a lateral façade corresponding to the billiard room on the

first floor. It also has a stained glass window by the A. Rigalt Company, who also created the rest of the stained glass for the building. The interior demonstrates a great decorative richness. Today it is the headquarters of the **Francisco Godia Foundation,** created in 1998 to gather together the collection of the businessman and art collector Francisco Godia Sales. It specialises in medieval art, ceramics, modernist paintings and drawings, as well as 20th Century art.

Passeig de Gràcia, 33
Escola de les Dames Negres (1916). See page 33-34.

Diagonal, 450
Church and convent of Pompeia (1910) the church, with its three naves separated by slender columns, picks up on aspects of traditional Catalan Gothic, such as the central nave with its arches containing wooden beams. The inventiveness of the architecture can be noted in the stylised floral capitals or in the triangular openings. The stone façade is notable for the work of the sculptor Josep Llimona, who created a relief on the door and an image of St Francis of Assisi above it. The Neo-Gothic convent is more sober, following the Franciscan tradition of humility; it combines stone with brickwork. It was founded by the Capuchin monk Rupert Maria de Manresa, a great admirer of the Italian sanctuary at Pompeii. The building was restored after the Spanish Civil War, with every attempt being made to reproduce the original look of the interior.

From València to Aragó

Numbers 66–56

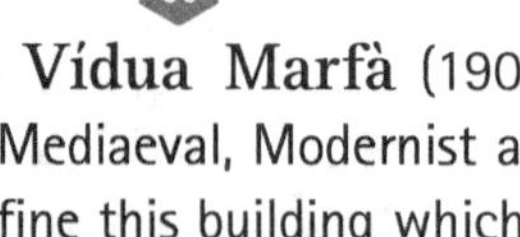

66

🏛 **Casa Vídua Marfà** (1905). A mix of Mediaeval, Modernist and Gothic define this building which is currently the head offices of the *Escola Superior de Relacions Públiques i Màrqueting* and the *Escola de Co-municació, Turisme i Empresa*, under the wing of the University of Barcelona. The building, designed by the architect Manuel Comas i Thos, has a spectacular entrance with three huge wooden doors carved with Gothic motifs and three great arches

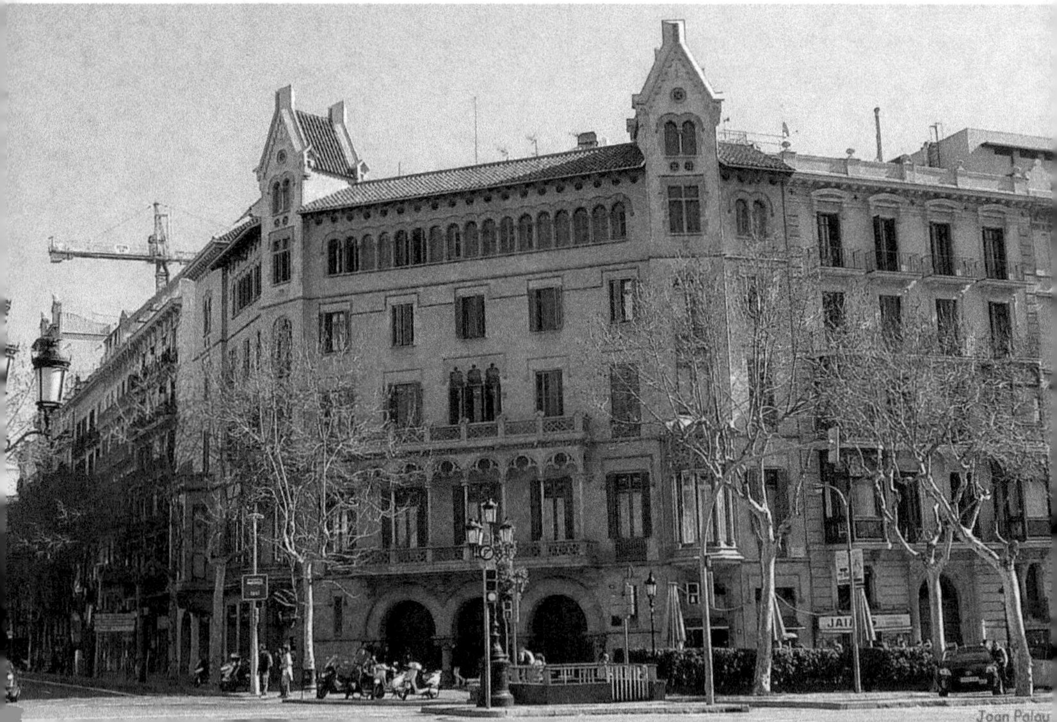

🛍️ **Timberland.** The 240 m² of this US company, founded in 1978, is dedicated to footwear, sports and mountaineering clothes and accessories; all manufactured with an absolute commitment to the environment. Timberland is committed to "Doing Well and Doing Good".

🏢 **Sixtyfour.** Exclusive luxury apartments. Completely refurbished, the apartments have from one to three rooms and large spaces where design, natural light and the quality of materials mark the priorities. Ideal for both families with children and groups of friends.

🛍️ **Tascón.** This brand was founded in 1959 by José Tascón and now has more than sixteen boutiques, shared between Barcelona and Madrid, offering men and women top brands in footwear: Clarks, Panama Jack, Camper or Nike, among others.

supported by thick stubby columns with floral capitals. The theme of arches and columns is continued in the lobby which gives access to two staircases and the splendid polychromatic glass skylight. On the façade, note the Gothic rostrum on the first floor, the upper gallery which stretches across the whole corner as well as the towers (finished off with pointed frontispieces and numerous gargoyles with animal motifs). Can you find a frog with teeth, or a monkey preening itself?

🛍️ **Sanremo.** The name is synonymous with famous brand perfumes, cosmetics and personal hygiene products, along with a hairdresser's.

🍴 **Caffé di Francesco.** A well-known chain of cafés with coffee from all over the world. It has rustic decorations and always brings to mind the aroma of a good cup of coffee, perhaps accompanied by a cake or pastry.

Casa del Llibre. See the "Of particular note" section, page 136.

Sixtytwo (4*). In the vestibule of this exclusive hotel you can already guess what you will find in the rest of the building: Moooi, Vitra, B&B or Philipe Starck. Its 45 rooms have Bang & Olufsen televisions, Jacob Jensen telephones or taps by Tangent. With an emphasis on design and modernist interiors from 1897, in a relaxing and cosmopolitan ambience, the hotel offers complimentary services such as wine and shopping routes, or massages to get you toned up, among others.

Casa Olano (1885). This house is also known as the **Pirate's House** or the **Edifici Elcano.** It is a 19th Century building, influenced by classicism, the work of Tiberi Sabater i Carner. Of particular note is its wide symmetrical façade and a niche containing a sculpture of the mariner Juan Sebastián Elcano, the work of Francesc Font. Plaques in Catalan and Basque commemorate the fact that this building was home to the Basque Delegation in Catalonia during the Spanish Civil War (1936-1939).

Replay. An Italian brand with more than 200 boutiques around the world, founded in 1981 by Claudio Buziol. Urban clothing for men, women and kids; also eyewear, underwear, footwear, accessories and perfumes. Of particular note is its spectacular interior decoration, already hinted at by the shop window with its vertical garden at the back. Later there is a splendid staircase to the first floor, a patio and a courtyard garden at the back.

Curious fact: The name for the brand came to the founder when he was watching an action replay from a football game on television.

Txapela. Here you can try the famous Basque *pinchos* (over 50 varieties of *pinchos)*, small portions of bread with some foodstuff on top, that have to be washed down with a delicious *xacolí* white wine, a glass of cider or with *zuritos* (little shots of beer in shallow glasses). The company have another restaurant at number 10.

La Baguetina Catalana. Fast-food, sandwiches and pizza slices for those on a reduced budget.

Burberry. This shop takes up the whole corner of *Carrer Aragó*, within a monumental building by the architect Joan Padrós, built in 1935 and refurbished in 2011. It sells

clothes, shoes, perfumes, watches, handbags and travel bags along with all kinds of accessories sporting the famous crest showing an English Knight riding an elegant charger. The company was founded in 1856.

Curious fact: It was built as the headquarters of the *Sociedad Anónima Cros*, one of the first entirely commercial buildings on the *Passeig*.

Carrer Aragó towards the Besós

Aragó, 282

Madrid-Barcelona. This well-known, refurbished restaurant in *Carrer Aragó* owes its name to the train to Madrid which used to thunder past it in the 1950s. In-season Catalan cuisine, excellent value for

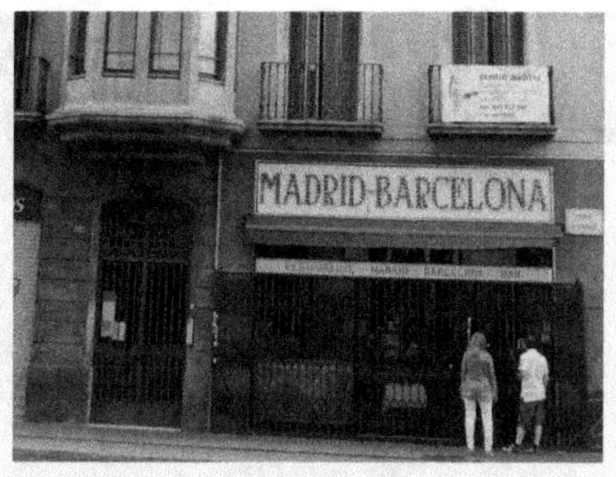

money and a welcoming and traditional atmosphere with a decoration fills of details.

From Aragó
to Consell de Cent

Numbers 54–44

54

 **Banco Pastor building** (1982). Designed by the architect Josep M. Fargas Falp, this singular, dun coloured building takes up the entire corner. It still sports its original name, although it is now a branch of the *Banco Popular* and an office block.

52

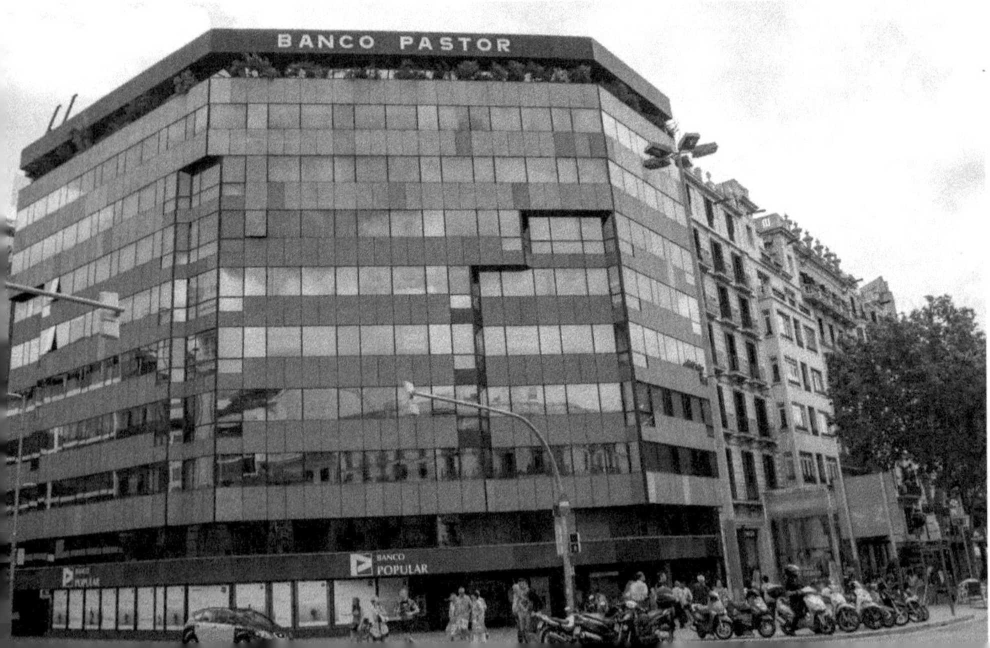

 **Geox.** *Geo*, in Greek, meant "earth". The X refers to technology. Set up in Italy in 1990, this 340 m^2 boutique with its warm colours and its elegant interior sells trousers, jackets and accessories for women, men, girls and boys, but also all kinds of shoes with a micro-porous

membrane in the rubber soul to allow transpiration, the source of this brand's success. Geox offers durability and protection style and comfort. They have another establishment at number 9-11.

🛍 **María Candelas.** Every kind of furniture or household article you could dream of can be found here. They have exclusive items they have designed themselves including their own perfume range, but also a selection of furniture, lighting and curtains, etc, by international brands including porcelain by Versace or glass decorated taps by Swarovski.

main floor which offers support to the gallery on the floor above and the broad railings linking all the balconies. Sculptures representing huge pitchers crown the balustrade on the rooftop terrace.

🏛 **Casa Casarramona** (1923). A work by the architect Josep Puig i Cadafalch, from his yellow period, when he had distanced himself from modernism, it uses a more sober and rationalist language. Of note are the wooden bay on the

🍴 **McDonald's.** The ground floor of the building houses a branch of the famous American fast-food chain which has changed its usual red for green, as it is more ecological and adapted to the times.

46

🛍 **Swarovski.** A white swan welcomes you to the frozen forest that is this magic and exclusive cut glass universe. Established in 1895 by the craftsman Daniel Swarovski, born in the kingdom of Bohemia, now in the Czech Republic, the fifth generation of the family continues to offer the public its celebrated glasswork: jewellery, accessories and lighting, among others. The highlight of this 84 m² shop is a lighting feature with more than 10,000 crystal pieces and the brilliant prism shapes covering the walls.

🛍 **Joieria Gràcia.** With origins going back to 1897, they have more than 30 years experience in selling and purchasing pre-owned watches and jewels.

44

🛍 **Philipp Plein.** Contemporary and cosmopolitan luxury from this German designer. Clothes and accessories for men, women and children. All concentrated in 210 m², shared over two levels. The light and shade playing over the white stone and mirrors highlight even further the

items on display. Most impressive is the great spider chandelier with crystal skulls by Murano and the huge skull made up of thousands of Swarovski crystals which dominates the entrance.

🍴 **Tapa Tapa.** "What would life be like without tapas?" That is the question asked by this restaurant chain. Another place in the city where you can choose from a menu with more than 50 different tapas inside or out on the terrace.

🍴 **Citrus.** On the first floor, on the corner with *Consell de Cent*. In 2008, national design winner, Toni Arola, created the warm contemporary look that envelops you as you enter the restaurant. Tones of wood, blacks, yellows and reds help you enjoy modern recipes and traditional Mediterranean dishes. Of note are the emblematic trio of citric sorbets and the star dish: the tomato and mozzarella skyscraper with olive paste and rocket salad. Live music on Thursdays.

Carrer Consell de Cent towards the River Besòs

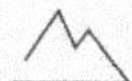

Consell de Cent, 355

Gioricky Concept Store. An outlet mall, next to *Passeig de Gràcia* specializing, above all, in Italian brands such as Just Cavalli, Dolce&Gabana, Tru Trussardi, Dsquared, Blauer or Gucci. There are also accessories from Balenciaga, Lanvin and their own brand. A must visit place for those wishing to purchase top brands at discounts between 40 and 60%.

Consell de Cent, 314

Agatha Ruiz de la Prada. Stars, flowers and hearts of every size and colour imaginable. Fun and daring clothes for men, women and children as well as accessories for the home; all in an environment in which the walls, ceilings and floors are of a striking magenta.

Consell de Cent, 320

Capdevila. An establishment with a long tradition in the city. Four generations of jewellers and silversmiths have worked in this Catalan jeweller's and silverware store since 1905. Contemporary jewellery, unique pieces, studies for projects and custom made items, along with the restoration of antique and modern jewels. **Curious fact:** Since 1956, this jeweller's has been commissioned with creating a jewel representing the letter *phi* in the Greek alphabet which is then offered as the *Lletra d'Or* prize awarded by jury to the best work written in Catalan in the previous year. Amongst those who have received the award are: Joan-Lluís Lluís, Júlia Guillamon, Josep M. Espinàs or Empar Moliner.

Consell de Cent, 324

Salvador Serra / Raig. Two historic establishments specialising in photography, as well as meteorological and astronomical instruments. They have left their original homes at *Passeig de Gràcia* 22 and *Plaça Catalunya* and have set up together in this new site where they continue offering analogue photographic services and instruments for measuring the weather or seeing the stars.

Looking earthwards: the *panots*

Walking down the *Passeig de Gràcia* it is natural to raise your eyes to view the historic buildings, luxury shops, traditional establishments, singular hotels and a rich and varied gastronomy. However, when we look towards the ground we find ourselves pleasantly surprised at something which we should not have overlooked: the paving stones known as the *panots*. The most famous of them, because it is the work of Anthony Gaudi, is a pavement created in 1904 by the Escofet factory that we can walk from one end of the boulevard to the other. This is comprised of four a half centimetres thick hexagonal paving stones in a grey green colour, popularly known as a *Gaudí mosaic*. Like much of the work of the celebrated Catalan architect, it demonstrates his detailed observation of nature. In this case, the mosaic (observable only if you combine various slabs together correctly) transports us to the bottom of the sea where sea snails, starfish or seaweed take shape before our eyes - some even claim to see an octopus. The reason Gaudi chose maritime motifs is because it was originally planned to place these slabs in front and in the interior of *Casa Batlló*, where the sea and water are omnipresent. However, finally, they were used in the *Casa Milà* and, later, along the whole *Passeig de Gràcia*. The only difference between the current paving slabs and the originals is that from 1997 onwards the original relief has been transformed into an engraving in order to improve their adherence as well as to enable them to cope better with wear over time. The Gaudí mosaic combines, in *Passeig de Gràcia* and the rest of Barcelona, with other equally characteristic paving slabs. The best known being the "Rose of Barcelona" which involves adding a circular round pink

coloured stone to indicate the **Modernism Route** (an itinerary that takes in the principal modernist buildings in the city). However, it is easy to find four other models: the slabs of chocolate, the four circles, the concentric circumferences and the rhombuses. All of them have the same measurements: 20 × 20 cm, and were manufactured by the Escofet Company. They have formed part of the city since 1916.

All these paving slab designs can be acquired in different sizes, shapes and styles stamped onto bags, boxes, chocolate bars and indeed any kind of product imaginable in the majority of souvenir shops in the city.

While looking earthwards, keep an eye out for green coloured slabs in front of certain trees. These reveal, in Catalan, Spanish and Latin, which tree we are looking at.

From Consell de Cent to Diputació

Numbers 42–32

42

🛍 **Miu Miu.** This was the first shop of the Prada group in Barcelona. The two floors have walls whose decoration evokes the feeling that you are inside a huge safe where, exposed as gems, you can acquire ready-to-wear collections, handbags, shoes, jewellery and accessories from the youngest granddaughter of Mario Prada.

🛍 **Llorenç.** This jeweller's is a guarantee of quality. Now run by the third generation of a Barcelona family which, since 1934, has offered the public their own exclusive items.

38 **40**

🛍 **Brioni.** Considered one of the best tailors in the world. Established in 1945, in Rome, since 1985 they have had their own tailoring school. They have 300 m² of space shared over three floors along with a lounge area where you can relax while they take your measurements.

Curious fact: This shop at number 65 was opened on the 65th anniversary of the company.

Mandarin Oriental (5*). One of the most exclusive and luxurious hotels in the city. Exclusivity and luxury are in the very air as you pass the columns at the entrance and glide up the long ramp into what was once the headquarters of the *Banco Hispano Americano*. It has 93 rooms and 27 suites with views of the *Passeig de Gràcia* and the interior gardens. Of particular note are the 236 m² penthouse suite on the top floor; the restaurant *Moments*, run by the prestigious Carme Ruscalleda (with 7 Michelin stars under her belt) and her son Raül Balam, and, it goes without saying, the interior gardens, the terrace and the swimming pool from which you can enjoy a privileged view of the city. It also has a luxury spa taking up 1000 m², with eight treatment booths, a swimming pool, a fitness centre and complementary services.

Tiffany's & Co. The only thing missing here is Audrey Hepburn having breakfast in the shop window. What this establishment is not missing is the luxury linked to the brand, nor the omnipresent and patented Tiffany Blue. There are three floors, connected by a spiralling light, separated by categories: high-class jewellery, engagement rings and contemporary jewellery. Exquisite attention to detail is the hallmark of this company.

Mango. The largest store in the city of this brand started by Catalan businessman Isak Andic. It has 1500 m² of space distributed over two floors, high ceilings, huge screens and carefully controlled lighting. Here you can find all the company's current lines: H.E. by Mango, Mango Touch, Mango Kids and Mango Sport & Intimates.

Punt Roma. Specialising in value for money clothes from sizes 38 to 54, their slogan is "fashion for all kinds of women".

Adolfo Domínguez. Chiaroscuro lighting accompanies charac-

teristic timeless and elegant clothes and accessories for the whole family. "Wrinkles are beautiful" was the company slogan in the 1980s. Today they have a presence in 42 countries. Their commitment to the environment is reflected in their creations: no exotic skins, bags made from recyclable material and the temperature in their shops.

 **Hostal Oliva** (2*). Although you would never guess it from the outside, once you have passed between the shop windows of Adolfo Domínguez and entered the lobby of the building you find yourself in a well lit inner courtyard, amongst extremely high ceilings, Doric columns, stately staircases and an antique wood panelled lift. On the fourth floor, is a simple, reasonably-priced, good-quality pension.

Carrer Diputació towards the River Besòs

Diputació, 269
Tapas 24. This is one of the many restaurants that the former chef from the world-famous *El Bulli*, Carles Abellán, has throughout the world. Here you can find, at reasonable prices, fresh produce and quality tapas in an informal and relaxed atmosphere.

Diputació, 273
Thai Barcelona. Their slogan says it all: *"Thai Barcelona. Royal Cuisine. It's a Thai garden!"* A place with the aromas, tastes and sensations to transport you directly to ancient Siam, surrounded by plants, goddesses and wood panels carved with Thai symbols. They also do takeaway food.

Diputació, 264
St. Moritz (4*). The building has been listed as a historical building since 1883. It has been a hotel since 1990 and was completely refurbished in 2010. It has 91 rooms with a mixture of stately Barcelona classicism and more contemporary elements.

From Diputació to Gran Via de les Corts Catalanes

Numbers 30–18

🛍 **Zara Home.** Almost 2000 m², on three levels, of items for the home in a shop in which the colour white and bright illumination are omnipresent.

🏛 **Casa Antoni i Marc Rocamora** (1913). A modernist building designed by the brothers Joaquim i Bonaventura Bassegoda Amigó, notable for its floral reliefs, the sinuous profiles of its balconies, the perforated feature on the crown and the dragon wrapping itself around the pinnacle on the corner.

🍴 **Divinus.** This restaurant fuses international and modern Mediterranean cuisine. It specialises in roasted meats with vegetables, in an urban and modern design and is good value for money. It also has outdoor tables.

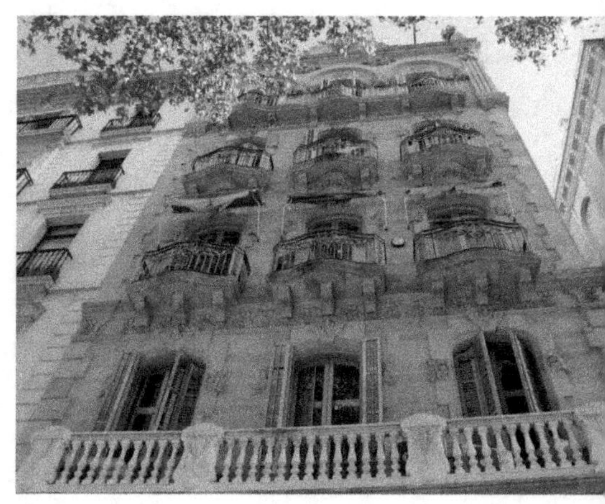

🛍 **Señor.** As its name indicates, this tailor's creates made-to-measure suits for men. They do this in only 10 days and have done so ever since Josep M. Ribas Prunés and Ignasi Closas Augé started their first business in Manresa in 1961. The brand has seven establishments and once made up to 15,000 suits in a year.

🍴 **El Nacional.** A gastronomic multi-space where you can enjoy traditional Spanish recipes: tapas, meats, fish, traditional Catalan *coques,* bonbons or bars specialising in wines, beers, cocktails, oysters or caviar. It can seat 770 diners and takes up 3,500 m² of an 8m high

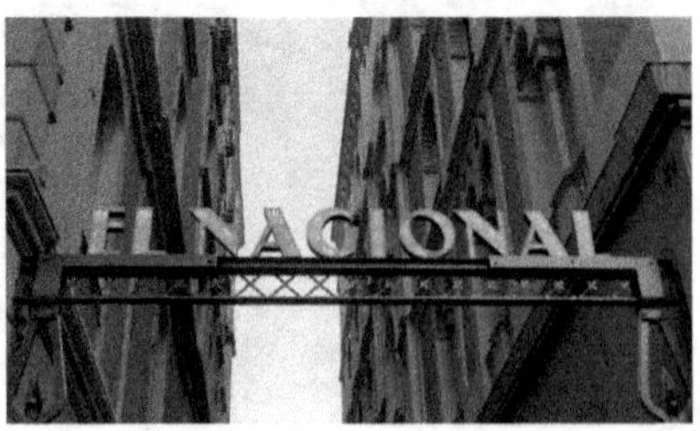

building with impressive domed ceilings; a Catalan style representative of 19th Century industrial architecture. **Curious fact:** Initially, there was a family home on the site, then, between 1840-1863, it became *El Criadero* a kind of beer garden, and between 1870-1900 it was the site of the *Teatro Español.* The current building once housed a cloth and dyes factory, then the first automobile dealership in the city. It has also been a car park, among other uses.

🏢 **Casa Pere Llibre** (1872). This is one of the few neo-Arabian styles houses left in Barcelona. Designed by the architect Domènec Balet i Nadal, the building originally had a twin on the opposite corner of the boulevard. In 1962, the ground floor was refurbished in an art deco style, very different from the rest of the building. Fortunately, we can still admire the Islamic influenced façade with its terracotta panels, its plasterwork with geometric forms and wrought iron railings on the balconies.

🍴 **Qu Qu.** These are the initials of *Quasi Queviures,* a restaurant that almost transports us back to an early 20th Century grocer's, since the decoration emulates a typical

moved to this current location. They owe their success to the quality of their fabrics and, above all, to their excellent personal contact with their customers.

apartment of the district of the *Eixample* with its hydraulic mosaic floors, touches of colour and huge windows. There are two dining rooms, a terrace and a special corner for Iberian ham and sausages (all home cooked like grandma would make it).

 Mango Kids. A boutique dedicated exclusively to quality children's fashion at a good price. It has some 430 m^2 for boys and girls from 3 to 12.

 Bel. One of the oldest tailor's in Barcelona. Their first shop opened in 1842 in the *Plaça Reial*. In 1940, they

 Tous. This shop, the official distributors for Rolex watches, is one of the 400 the company has in 45 countries. On sale are jewellery, bags, perfumes, accessories and, of course, their celebrated teddy bears, created in 1985 by Rosa Oriol. On this spot once stood the historic jeweller's J. Roca, founded in 1888, which closed in 2008 due to a retirement. The façade and the inte-

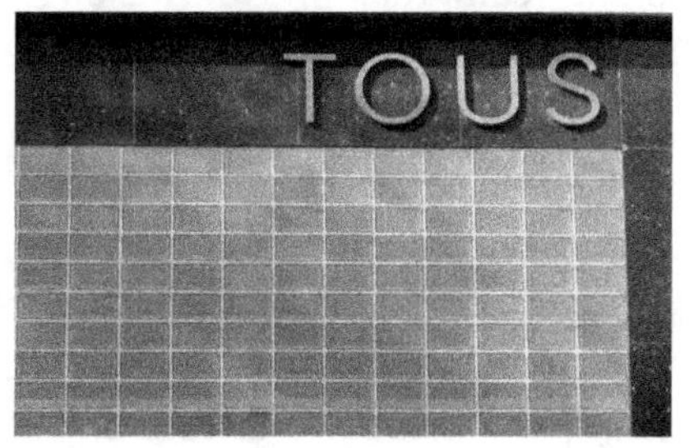

rior, in a rationalist style, were designed by the architect Josep Lluís Sert, in 1934. They have another establishment at number 75.

Subway. One of a chain of fast food restaurants that you can find anywhere in the world, especially if you cross the Atlantic. The story begins in Bridgeport, US, in 1965, and now they have more than 42,700 establishments spread across 108 countries and they are famous for their sandwiches, salads and above all for their submarine sandwich, popularly known as a "Sub", filled with meat, sausages, cheeses, vegetables and various sauces.

Gran Via de les Corts Catalanes: towards the River Besòs

Gran Via de les Corts Catalanes, 636

The North Face. US firm specialising in sports clothes, footwear and equipment for skiing, snowboarding, mountaineering, hiking and backpacking or trail running. Since 1968, it has seen its logos crossing every imaginable terrain, from the summit of Everest, where the brand really took off, to ski slopes, Amazonian forests, ocean crossings, or walks along the *Passeig de Gràcia* in the rain. They are particularly famous for their waterproof wear with HydroSeal and Gore-Tex fabrics.
Curious fact: North Face's logotype is inspired by the North face of the Half Dome, in Yosemite Valley, California.

Gran Via de les Corts Catalanes, 642

Menkes. A benchmark for other stores selling and hiring costumes and accessories. Since 1950, they have provided outfits for every event imaginable. Flamenco dresses? Menkes has them in spades. Tuxedos? Of course; as well as clothes for dance and theatre, or superhero costumes.

Gran Via de les Corts Catalanes, 644

HC Passeig de Gràcia (4*). A hotel with 74 rooms in a neoclassical style building. It has a swimming pool, a solarium and all the other services associated with 4 stars.

The smart *Passeig de Gràcia*

Barcelona's City Hall, the *Ajuntament*, has decided to convert the *Passeig de Gràcia* into the first Smart Street in the city. Technology (including sensors and fibre optics) installed at a series of strategic points along the boulevard allows for the gathering of data which is used to improve municipal services and resources. For example, the street lighting along the boulevard can be regulated in accordance with the flow of pedestrians, or traffic, or the level of atmospheric pollution. The quality of water in public drinking fountains can be monitored or the level of noise pollution coming from a terrace or a particular spot. These initiatives are ongoing and have led to an improvement in services such as rubbish collection, irrigation, illumination or traffic flow.

In addition, the installation of Wi-Fi nodes offers free Internet access for visitors, who can locate restaurants, hotels or boutiques or consult the timetables of museums and exhibitions or public transport in the area on their smart phones whenever they wish: all of the information, available to everyone.

Bookshops

There is also room for books on the *Passeig de Gràcia*. Novels, poetry, essays, guidebooks, maps, magazines, dictionaries or electronic books can be easily found in the bookshops along the boulevard or in the streets surrounding it.

Casa del Llibre (Passeig de Gràcia, 62). Founded in 1923, the *Casa del Llibre* (house of books) has seven bookshops in Barcelona. These specialise in every kind of material imaginable with a wide selection of latest additions, specialist tomes on music and cinema and electronic books.

Jaimes (València, 318) is Barcelona's French bookshop, just a few metres from *Passeig de Gràcia*. Here you can buy books in French, Catalan, Spanish, English, Italian and Portuguese. It organises roundtables, presentations, conferences and exhibitions. From 1951 until 2013, it was one of the traditional bookshops on the *Passeig de Gràcia*. Now, on *Carrer València*, it continues to offer the latest in French literature and essay, as well as having an extensive, well chosen and pampered children's section.

Documenta (Pau Claris, 144): From 1975 to 2014, it was one of the main bookshops in the old centre of the city. Now on the *Eixample*, it has begun a new lease of life with all the rigour, professionalism and affability it was famous for. In addition to all the latest literature, it has a conscientious selection of works on art, humanities, history, anthropology and philosophy. It is the ideal place for those looking for specialised advice and assistance.

Laie (Pau Claris, 85): its slogan says it all "Laie, the pleasure of culture"; as does its logo showing a cup of steaming coffee on top of a book. For this is a two-storey bookshop-cafe-restaurant with a patio that is ideal for reading, resting and relaxing. It has a careful selection of both national and foreign new books on a wealth of subjects.

Altair (Gran Via, 616) is a bookshop specialising in travel, excursions, anthropology and nature; its two floors containing all kinds of information for travellers. The atmosphere is relaxed, with chairs and tables where you can read without any haste.

From Gran Via de les Corts Catalanes to Casp

Numbers 16-6

16

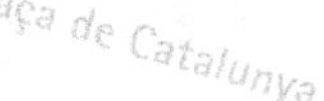 **Banco Rural y Mediterráneo building** (1953). The commission that architect Agustí Borrell Sensat received was to imitate the building on the opposite corner, the *Banco Vitalicio* (currently the *Generali*), a fact that can be appreciated if you compare the two buildings. The top two floors, which stand out from the rest of the building, were known as the Martini Terrace and were open to the public for many years. At the entrance, note the stone reliefs and the imposing Corinthian columns.

Zara. The ground floor of the building houses an emblematic shop for the whole family where you can find all the firm's collections. Zara Woman at the entrance, *Trafaluc* at the back, Zara Kids on one side, Zara for Men on the upper floor and Zara Home on the lower floor.

🏛 **Casas Rocamora** (1920). These three adjoining buildings, which stretch from number 12 to the corner of *Carrer Casp*, were joined together under the same façade by the architects and brothers Joaquim and Bonaventura Bassegoda Amigó. The group shows a marked neo-Gothic style with mediaeval references. On the façade there are four series of bays with balconies, pinnacles that rise above the railings of the terrace and four domes. Right on the corner, there is a circular tower with pinnacles which crowns the building. Like the domes, the roofs of the towers are made with ceramic scale-like tiles in an orange colour that contrasts with the white stone of the façade.

🛍 **Furest.** A family firm dedicated to fashion for men. In 1898, Estanislau Furest opened a shop on the *Plaça Reial* in the historical city center, and in 1917 moved it to the *Passeig de Gràcia*, where it became essential for anyone looking for quality made-to-measure shirts. The firm's logo is: "A place to cultivate a way of life". It also offers shoes, perfumes and gift and travel articles from leading brands. Not forgetting an area for functional clothes for women. It currently has seven stores in the city of Barcelona.

🛍 **& Other Stories.** This is the seventh boutique this brand has in Europe. Decorated in a New York style, in omnipresent white, it has 600 m² distributed over three floors.

Here you can acquire clothes, jewellery, accessories, bags, footwear, beauty products and access their tailoring facilities for men and women.

🍴 **Txapela.** A twin establishment of that at number 58, where you can continue to enjoy, inside or on the terrace, celebrated Basque food at reasonable prices: Xacolí wines, *pinchos, zuritos* of beer or glasses of cider.

 **6**

🛍 **Emporio Armani.** The boutique of one of Italy's most prestigious designers, Giorgio Armani. A giant screen welcomes you, displaying some of the firm's contributions to fashion shows. There are 620 m^2 spread over three floors, on which you can find complete collections for men and women, along with underwear

and swimwear, jewellery and a whole range of accessories. But you can also buy the brand's chocolates, preserves and teas in their delicatessen.

🛍 **Felgar.** The brand's name was extracted from the name of the founder, FELicitas GARcés Broto. It is a family business now in its third generation, founded in 1963, which offers leading fashion brands for women from DKNY to Armani, through Michael Kors, Twin-Set, Aldo Martins or Liu-Jo.

Carrer Casp towards the Besòs

Carefully crossing *Carrer Casp*, turn towards the distant River Besòs. From here you can see, beyond the *Eixample*, the majestic and colourful *Torre Agbar*. Designed by the architect Jean Nouvel it was inaugurated in 2005. A thirty-one storey building, it is 142 metres tall and is covered in 59,619 glass panels.

Casp, 1-13

 Barcelona Atiram (4*). An establishment that is close to everywhere, it has 79 rooms. From its terrace on the seventh floor you can enjoy impressive panoramic views of *Plaça Catalunya*. It has rooms for meetings and events.

Casp, 19

 Mussol. A restaurant where you can enjoy Catalan cuisine with specialities such as in-season vegetables and meats prepared to traditional recipes.

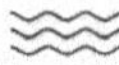

Casp, 2

 Bracafé. Since 1929, this coffee bar has provided a meeting place in the centre of the city for Barcelona's inhabitants. Drinking a quality coffee or having a beer and a bite has always been a treat in this traditional nook, far from the traffic which roars past just a few metres away on the *Passeig*.

Casp, 8

 Teatro Tívoli (1849). It began life as the *Tivoli Gardens* in 1849, under the direction of Bernat-Agustí de Las Cases. There is evidence of an open-air "summer theatre" here that led to the construction of a theatre building in 1880. However, the current building, on the same site, dates back to 1919. This theatre, in a neo-rococo style can seat 1,643, although it still maintains some of its original elements such as the moulds, floral motifs in gold and red, the plush seats and the curtains. Of particular note is the canopy in steel, glass and light bulbs at the main entrance.

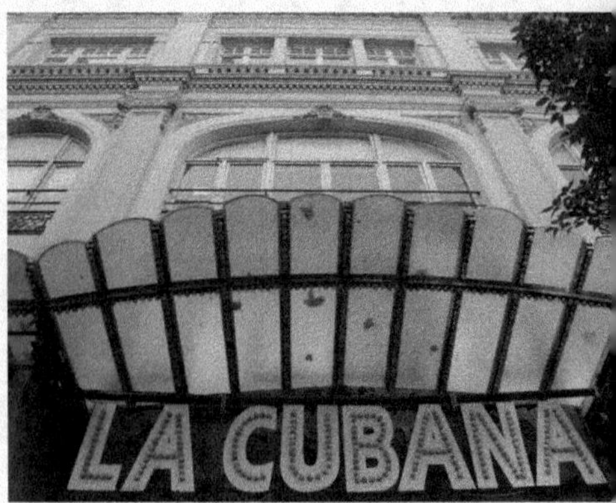

From Casp
to Ronda de Sant Pere

Numbers 4-2

4 2

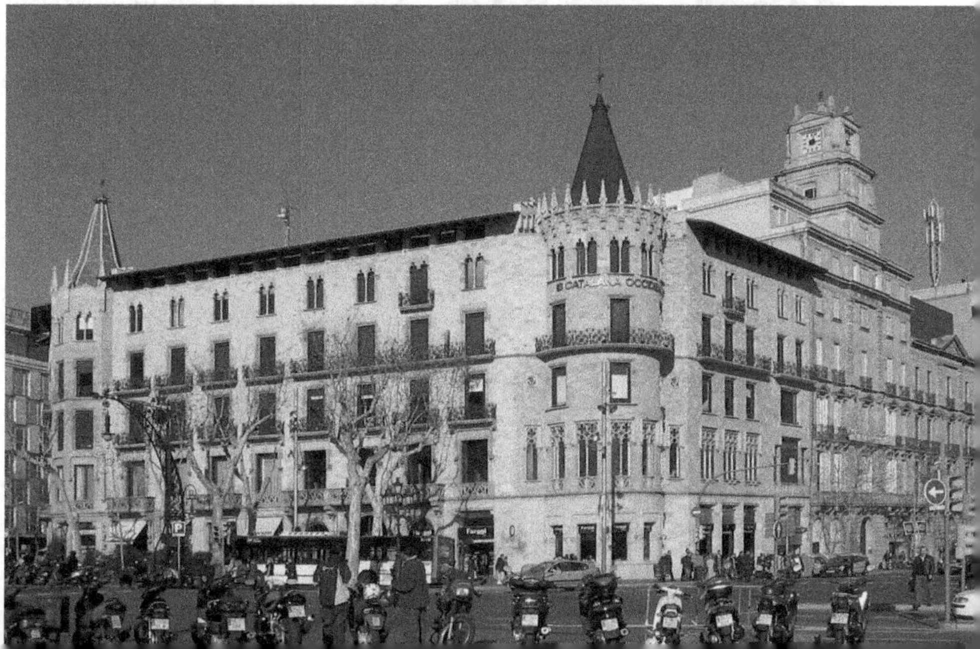

 **Casa Pascual i Pons** (1891). Designed by Enric Sagnier i Villavecchia, this was the first modernist building on the *Passeig de Gràcia*. In fact, these were two independent homes built for the families of Sebastià Pascual and Alexandre Pons, unified through the same image. Of note are the neo-Gothic forms on the façade, the generalised use of stone, the floral touches on the windows and towers (one circular and the other polygonal; each finished off with a steeple and pinnacles on the cornice). At the main entrance to number 2, you can appreciate the rich ornamentation of the original, the fireplace and the stained glass. The

interiors are enriched with furniture from Germany and with contributions from craftsmen and artists, among which the most notable are the stained glass by Rigalt i Granell or the painted tapestries by Alexandre de Riquer.

🍴 **Navarra.** Situated on the corner with *Carrer Casp*, this restaurant serves up local Catalan dishes along with those from Navarre and the Basque Country. Surrounded by wood and under the great glass skylight on the ceiling, we recommend you try the goat's cheese salad, the sirloin steak and the almond puff pastry.

🛍 **Swatch.** In 1983, they revolutionised the plastic watch-making sector by producing watches with 51 pieces, when traditionally they had been made with 91.

🍴 **Dino.** An ice cream parlour established in 1978 by the Italian Dino Pavese which now has 45 establishments in Catalonia and the Balearic Is-

lands. They have flavours from classics like vanilla, cream or chocolate, to specialities like *stracciatella*, Roquefort or ice-cream for those on a special diet.

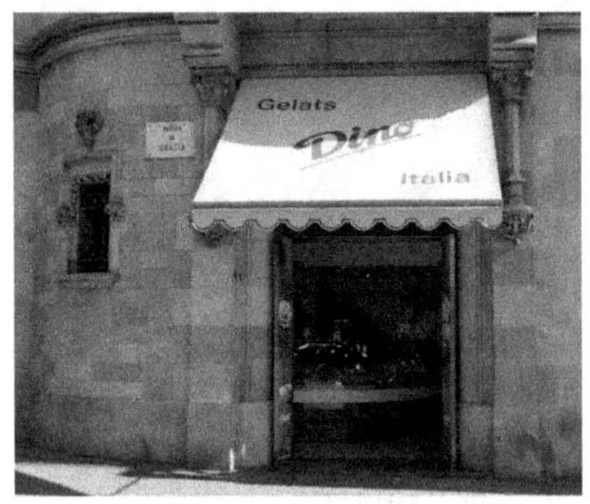

🛍 **Punt 1995.** A shop dedicated to women's fashion and knitting accessories.

🛍 **Camper.** The second store on the *Passeig de Gràcia* belonging to this Mallorcan shoemaker's (the other is at number 100). Modern boutiques that are simple but innovative where you can find footwear for men, women and children.

🍴 **Farggi Café.** A Catalan ice cream parlour with more than 60 branches which emerged from the Farga pastry makers. Here you can try ice creams or coffees and teas with cakes, among other items. All of the highest quality, and all under the umbrella of their three mottos: satisfaction, leadership and excellence.

Plaça de Catalunya

This square of almost five hectares is considered the neuralgic centre of Barcelona and marks the meeting point of the old city, the district of *Ciutat Vella*, and the major expansion known as the *Eixample*.

The square's history goes back to mediaeval times when this area, just outside the walls of the city, was the starting point for the main routes out of the city and a meeting place for merchants. It was not until the city walls were demolished, in the middle of the 19th Century, that

it became the square we recognise today when the expansion plan of engineer and urban planner Ildefons Cerdà was put into operation and the city grew around it. Then, as now, it was a place where everything began and finished, a fine place for a meeting point from which you can begin to discover the city and from which the main urban and interurban transport facilities leave. The central area of the square, with its

famous for mass political actions; in May 2011, the square was occupied by the tents and bivouacs of the "*indignats*" (part of the "occupy" movement) which took over the square pacifically for nearly a month in order to bring attention to the economic political and social crisis that had begun in 2008.

huge star, is a common place to hold cultural activities, particularly during the three-day public party known as the *Festa Major* of the city. It is also

We would like to suggest a route which begins in *Passeig de Gràcia*, looking towards the sea and continues in a clockwise direction.

Ronda de Sant Pere towards the River Besòs

Ronda de Sant Pere, 3-5

La Sud América building. One of two buildings on *Plaça Catalunya* to have a clock. It also has some phrases sculpted into the façade from when the building be-

longed to the insurance company *La Sud América Seguros*: "La fe fortalece" (Faith fortifies), "La esperanza vivifica" (Hope gives life), "La caridad ennoblece" (Charity ennobles) and "El trabajo dignifica" (Work dignifies). The building was built for banker and politician, Manuel Girona.

14

🛍 **El Corte Inglés.** A department store located between the *Ronda de Sant Pere* and *Carrer de Fontanella* with an interesting story behind it. On this site, in the 1930s, stood the Military Casino of Barcelona. In the 1940s, after the Civil War, it was home to the restaurant and ballroom the *Salón Rigat* a place where only the best-off could afford to go. The department store was opened in 1962, coinciding with the celebrations of Barcelona's patron saint the *Festes de la Mercè*. It represented a breath of fresh air on a grey *Plaça Catalunya* which was otherwise full of insurance offices. In 1992, the architect Oriol Bohigas was commissioned to entirely refurbish the building as we see it today. The reforms received numerous criticisms, but also the FAD award for architecture and design. The store has a huge supermarket in the basement and a restaurant on the ninth floor with views of the *Plaça*.

Carrer Fontanella

Fontanella, 17

Casa de la estilográfica. Founded in 1938, here you can find everything pen-related from the items themselves to new cartridges and accessories by all the brands: Montblanc, Pelikan, Faber-Castell, Cross, Omas, etc. They also do repairs.

Fontanella, 20

Mil. Founded in 1917, although its origins go back to 1815, it is the leading hat suppliers in the city. It is difficult not to stop in front of their shop window piled with hats of all kinds: berets, Panama hats, airmen's flying helmets or top hats. There are hats for every occasion, whether a wedding, a carnival or a more serious event; and they only stock the best brands and materials.

Fontanella, 2

Mobile World Center Barcelona. A part-public, part-private initiative aimed at broadening public knowledge about mobile telephones and the Internet. There is a permanent exhibition displaying the latest trends and a timetable of activities which run from competitions and presentations to leisure and cultural activities.

Portal de l'Àngel

The spectacular illuminated thermometer on Cottet's optician's, dating back to 1956, welcomes shoppers to one of the other commercial axes of the city: the *Avinguda del Portal de l'Àngel*. This is a pedestrian street with a wide range of shops.

17

🏛 💳 **Banco de España.** This sombre and immense building has stood on the southern side of the square since 1957. It is ten stories high, with a total area of about 28,000 m², and was one of the first great concrete structures in the city, the work of architect Juan de Zavala. The ground and first floor are lined in granite, but the rest the building, with its austere marine and industrial motifs, is faced with the characteristic grey stone from the mountain of Montjuïc.

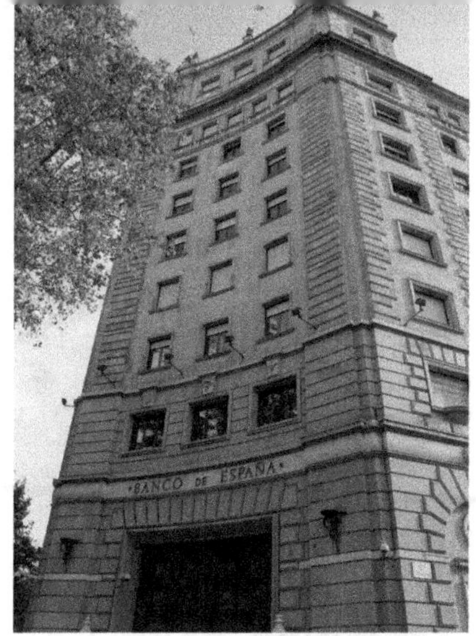

17 (basement)

ⓘ **Barcelona's Tourist Information Office.** This is the main tourist office in Barcelona, with 700 m² of space dedicated to providing visitors with all kinds of information about accommodation or travel within the city, or maps and pamphlets promoting tourist sites. You can access it by going down the stairs in the square in front of the *Corte Inglés* store.

Opening hours: daily: 8:30-20:30h. 26th of December and 6th of January, 9–15h
Closed: 1st of January and 25th of December
Information: 932 853 834
info@barcelonaturisme.com
www.barcelonaturisme.com

Bus: 16, 17, 24, 41, 42, 55, 58
Metro: L1, L3 (Catalunya)
FGC: (railway) Catalunya
Renfe: (railway) Plaça Catalunya, Passeig de Gràcia

19

🍴 **Farggi.** A Catalan ice cream parlour with an outdoor terrace on the street. Here you can enjoy fine quality ices, coffees, teas and pastries among other items. All of the highest quality.

🏨 **Olivia Plaza** (4*). A hotel with 113 modern and well-lit rooms which range from simple double rooms up to suites with a terrace. Of note is their bar and restaurant "Nineteen", from where you get fine views of the Church of Santa Anna.

20

🛍 **Alain Afflelou.** A franchise of this optician's founded in 1972 in Bordeaux, famous for their boast: a second pair of glasses for only €1 more.

21

🍴 **Hard Rock Café.** Typical American dishes and decoration to the sound of rock. This branch opened in 1997 and despite its recent whiter and more modern redecoration, it continues to maintain its own style. While you chomp on your nachos or hamburgers you can gaze at examples of Shakira's dresses, Madonna's corsets, Bruce Springsteen's jackets, or Freddy Mercury's shirts, among many other objects often donated by the artists themselves.

Carrer de Rivadeneyra

The end of this street offers a surprise, on the left there is a small peaceful square where you can escape from the noise emanating from *Plaça Catalunya*. And there is more, at the back of the square, some stairs lead down to the entrance to the monastery of Santa Anna, notable for its 12th Century church with Romanesque and Gothic elements, declared a national treasure. It retains its original Romanesque structure, with its basic cross shape and its square apse, covered in the 13th Century by a pointed barrel vault. The Gothic door is from 1300. In the adjacent square there is an ancient transept.

23

Antique Banca Arnús (1927) / El Corte Inglés.
See the "Sagnier Route" section, pages 116-117.

La Rambla

The most popular street in Barcelona begins at this point on *Plaça Catalunya* and rambles down to the port. With its great central avenue beneath the shade of hundred-year-old plane trees and a lane for cars on either side, it is full of stalls selling newspapers, flowers, ice creams and sweets. By tradition, if visitors wish to ever return to the city they must drink water from the *Canaletes* drinking fountain, at the top of the street, a few metres from the entrance to the Metro (Catalunya).

Carrer Pelai

Another of the popular commercial streets in the city leading to *Plaça Catalunya*. It has hotels, all kinds of shops and eating houses and is also a good way to wander down to the *Plaça de la Universitat* , the district of *Sant Antoni* and the left bank of the *Eixample*.

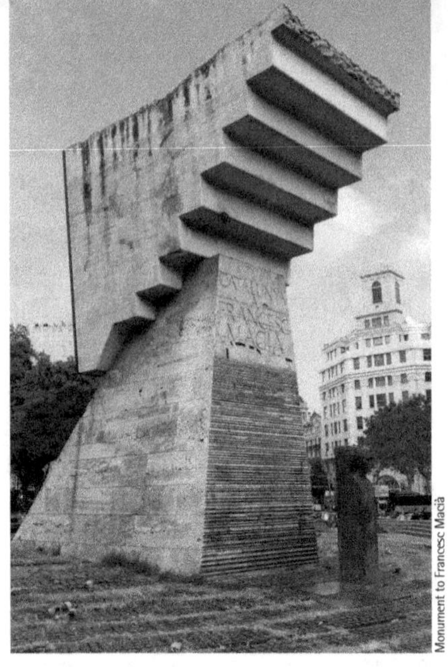

Monument to Francesc Macià

1

🛍 **El Triangle.** A large shopping mall with places to eat and various shops, among which the most notable is **FNAC,** part of a French chain specialising in books and technological and leisure appliances. It also has a salon where new books are presented and musicians can perform.

🍴 **Café Zurich.** This is surely the best-known cafe-bar in Barcelona and is a common city centre meeting point for both tourists and local inhabitants. Despite major reforms, it still retains its charm and a certain 19th Century style. Has a broad and highly popular terrace.

2-4

🛍 **Solaris.** Sunglasses from all brands in all styles and colours. Created in 1994, the company now has more than 400 sales points throughout the world.

Carrer Bergara

Bergara, 8

Pulitzer (4*). A hotel with ninety-two rooms totally equipped with the latest technologies and decorated using the most up-to-date materials. During the spring and summer they open the Pulitzer Terrace and offer live music and some beautiful views of the city.

Bergara, 4

Regina Hotel (4*). A elegant establishment, built in 1917, it has a modernist elements, but has learned how to adapt itself to the new times. It demonstrates a combination of timeless elegance and contemporary design. Of particular note is the canopy at the entrance.

Bergara, 11

Catalonia Plaza Catalunya (4*). This modernist hotel dates from 1899. It was designed by Antoni Gaudí's teacher, the architect Emilio Salas i Cortés. The hotel has all the facilities you would expect in its category, but also has a spa and a swimming pool in its inner courtyard.

Bergara, 5

Casa Agustí. Cooking for Barcelona since 1936. Despite various refurbishments, the decoration retains the nostalgic, welcoming and family ambience that has always characterised it. The menu offers typical Catalan dishes, most notably high quality fish and meats.

6

🏛 💳 **BBVA building** (1952). This building, which the BBVA bank rents, has 13,875 m² and is best known for the clock which rotates above its terrace. The clock was inaugurated in 1971: it is 4.7 meters in diameter, weighs 1,844 kilograms and the minute hand is 2 meters long.

7

🏨 **H10 Catalunya Plaza** (3*). A hotel located in a 19th Century building that was totally refurbished in 2013 and converted into a "Boutique Hotel". It is well located and designed and offers good service.

Ronda de la Universitat

Ronda de la Universitat, 37

🛍 **FCB Official Store.** The official shop of FC Barcelona, it sells T-shirts, jackets, caps, balls, towels

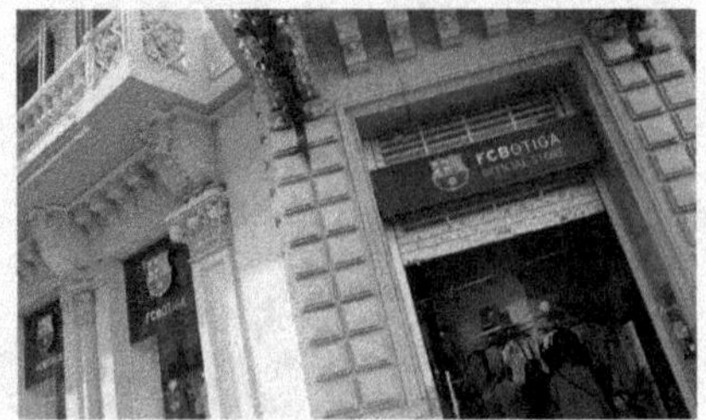

and many other objects from the *blaugrana* universe. FC Barcelona is "more than a club" in Catalonia.

Ronda de la Universitat, 35

🍴 **Milano Cocktail-Bar.** A classic and relaxing cocktail bar in which every day, after noon, you can travel back to the 1940s. Cocktails from the films and live jazz every day throughout the year. For lovers of good meat there is the famous steak tartar by Angel Martín.

9

🏛 **Casa Joan Pich i Pon** (1921). A sober building with classic lines and little concession to ornament, from the yellow period of Josep Puig i Cadafalch. Of particular note is the Baroque styled entrance, the temple-like pavilions crowning the angles of the corners and the statue of Hermes crowning the entire building, which gives the whole thing a monumental character.

🏛 **Public art.** Plaça de Catalunya is notable for the number of sculptures on display there. There is *La Deessa* (the goddess) by Josep Clarà (1878-1958), sat just in front of the *Monument to Francesc Macià* by Josep Maria Subirachs (1927-2014) representing two staircases, one on top of the other, then *Barcelona* by Frederic Marés (1893-1991) or *El Pastor* (the shepherd) by Pablo Gargallo (1881-1934).

In addition, scattered around the perimeter, are sculptures by Vicenç Navarro, Josep Dunyach, Eusebi Arnau, Josep Llimona, Josep Viladomat, Enric Casanovas, Josep Clarà, Antoni Parera, Jaume Otero, Joan Borrell, Llucià i Miquel Oslé, Jaume Duran, Josep Tenas and Enric Monjo.

The ornamental fountains in the square were the work of Fernando Espiau Seoane and were inaugurated in 1959.

Indexes

Uterque, Passeig de Gràcia, 65
934872010, www.uterque.com
Valentino, Passeig de Gràcia, 108
933683219, www.valentino.com
Vinçon, Passeig de Gràcia, 96
932156050, www.vincon.com
Wolford, Passeig de Gràcia, 104
933484251, www.wolfordshop.es
Yves Saint Laurent, Passeig de Gràcia, 102
932003955, www.ysl.com
Zadig & Voltaire, Passeig de Gràcia, 73
934676329, www.zadig-et-voltaire.com
Zara, Passeig de Gràcia, 16, 933187675, www.zara.com
Zara Home, Passeig de Gràcia, 30
933041292, www.zarahome.com

Museums / Art Galleries

Casa Batlló, Passeig de Gràcia, 43
932160306, www.casabatllo.es
Casa Lleó Morera, Passeig de Gràcia, 35
936762733, www.casalleomorera.com
Fundació Antoni Tàpies, Aragó, 255
934870315, www.fundaciotapies.org
Fundació Catalunya–La Pedrera, Passeig de Gràcia, 92
932142539, www.fundaciocatalunya-lapedrera.com
Fundació Frederic Mompou, Passeig de Gràcia, 108
932181481, www.fundaciomompou.cat
Fundació Institut Amatller d'Art Hispànic, Passeig de
Gràcia, 41, 934961245, www.amatller.org
Fundació Suñol, Passeig de Gràcia, 98
934961032, www.fundaciosunol.org
Galeria Comas, Passeig de Gràcia, 114
934153299, www.galeriacomas.com
Galeria Jordi Barnadas, Consell de Cent, 347
932156365, www.barnadas.com
La Pedrera / Casa Milà, Passeig de Gràcia, 92
902202138, www.lapedrera.com
Museu de la Perruqueria, Rambla de Catalunya, 99
932052419, www.museumraffelpages.com
Museu del Perfum, Passeig de Gràcia, 39
932160121/932160146, www.museudelperfum.com
Museu Egipci, València, 284
934880188, www.museuegipci.com
Palau Robert, Passeig de Gràcia, 107
932388091/92/93, www.gencat.cat/palaurobert
Sala Dalmau, Consell de Cent, 349
932154592, www.saladalmau.com

Singular Buildings

The former Banca Arnús, Plaça Catalunya, 23
Banco de España, Plaça Catalunya,17
Barcelona Stock Exchange, Passeig de Gràcia, 19
Can Serra, Rambla de Catalunya, 126,

Casa Amatller, Passeig de Gràcia, 41
Casa Ángel Batlló, Mallorca 253-257
Casa Antoni i Marc Rocamora, Passeig de Gràcia, 26
Casa Bonaventura Ferrer, Passeig de Gràcia, 113
Casa Casarramona, Passeig de Gràcia, 48
Casa Casas-Carbó, Passeig de Gràcia, 96
Casa Codina, Passeig de Gràcia, 94
Casa Coma, Passeig de Gràcia, 74
Casa Comalat, Avinguda Diagonal, 442
Casa Enric Batlló, Passeig de Gràcia, 75
Casa Fuster, Passeig de Gràcia, 132
Casa Garriga, Passeig de Gràcia, 112
Casa Jacint Esteva, Passeig de Gràcia, 104-108
Casa Joan Pich i Pon, Plaça Catalunya, 9
Casa Josefina Bonet, Passeig de Gràcia, 39
Casa Josep Arús, Rosselló, 240
Casa Josep Borràs, Passeig de Gràcia, 77
Casa Julià, Passeig de Gràcia, 80,
Casa Lleó Morera, Passeig de Gràcia, 35
Casa Lluís Ferrer-Vidal, Passeig de Gràcia, 114
Casa Malagrida, Passeig de Gràcia, 27
Casa Milà / La Pedrera, Passeig de Gràcia, 92
Casa Mulleras, Passeig de Gràcia, 37
Casa Olano / Elcano, Passeig de Gràcia, 60
Casa Pascual i Pons, Passeig de Gràcia, 2-4
Casa Pere Llibre, Passeig de Grácia, 24
Casa Puig Colom, Passeig de Gràcia, 7
Casa Ramon Servent, Gran de Gràcia, 7
Casa Terrades / Les Punxes, Avinguda Diagonal, 416-420
Casa Vídua Marfà, Passeig de Gràcia, 66
Casas Jofre, Passeig de Gràcia, 65
Casas Rocamora, Passeig de Gràcia, 6-14
Banco Español de Crédito building, Plaça Catalunya, 1
Banco Pastor building, Passeig de Gràcia, 54
Banco Rural y Mediterráneo building, Passeig de Gràcia, 16
BBVA building, Plaça Catalunya, 6
Union des Assurances de Paris building, Passeig de Gràcia, 33
Deutsche Bank building, Passeig de Gràcia, 111
Femina building, Passeig de Gràcia, 23
Generali building, Plaça Catalunya, 11
La Sud América building, Ronda de Sant Pere, 3-5
La Unión y el Fénix building, Passeig de Gràcia, 21
Publi building, Passeig de Gràcia, 55-57
Church and convent of Pompeia, Avinguda Diagonal, 450
Palau Baró de Quadras, Avinguda Diagonal, 373
Marcet Palace, Passeig de Gràcia, 13
Palau Robert, Passeig de Gràcia, 107

Restaurants / Bars

Barcelona Atiram, Casp, 1-13
933025858, www.barcelonaatiramhotels.com
Boca Chica, Passatge de la Concepció, 12
934675149, www.bocagrande.cat
Boca Grande, Passatge de la Concepció, 12
934675149, www.bocagrande.cat

Hotels

Bcn Design, Passeig de Gràcia, 29-31
933444555, www.eurostarsbcndesign.com
Casa Fuster, Passeig de Gràcia, 132
932553000, www.hotelescenter.es
Casa Gracia Barcelona Hostel, Passeig de Gràcia, 116
931874497/931740528, www.casagraciabcn.com
Catalonia Plaza Catalunya, Bergara, 11
933015151, www.hoteles-catalonia.com
Condes de Barcelona, Passeig de Gràcia 73
934450000, www.condesdebarcelona.com
Cristal palace, Diputació, 257
933930970, www.eurostarscristalpalace.com
El Palauet Living Barcelona, Passeig de Gràcia, 113
932180050, www.elpalauet.com
Equity Point Centric Hostel, Passeig de Gràcia, 113
93.231.20.45, www.equity-point.com
Gallery Hotel, Rosselló, 249
934159911/934159184, www.galleryhotel.com
H10 Catalunya Plaza, Plaça Catalunya, 7
933177171, www.hotelh10catalunyaplaza.com
HC Passeig de Gràcia, Gran Via de les Corts Catalanes,
644, 932702735, www.hoteles-catalonia.com
Hostal Oliva, Passeig de Gràcia, 32
934880162, www.hostaloliva.com
Majestic Hotel & Spa, Passeig de Gràcia, 68-70
934881717, www.hotelmajestic.es
Majestic Residence, Passeig de Gràcia, 69
934881717, www.majesticresidence.es
Mandarin Oriental, Passeig de Gràcia, 38-40
931518888, www.mandarinoriental.com
Olivia Plaza, Plaça Catalunya, 19
933168700, www.oliviaplazahotel.es
Omm, Rosselló, 265, 934454000, www.hotelomm.es
Paseo de Gràcia, Passeig de Gràcia, 102
932150603, www.hotelpaseodegracia.es
Pulitzer, Bergara, 8, 934816767, www.hotelpulitzer.es
Regina Hotel, Bergara, 4
933013232, www.reginahotel.com/es
Rocamora Apartments, Passeig de Gràcia, 51
933017561, www.rocamoraapartments.com
Royal Passeig de Gràcia, Passeig de Gràcia, 84
937370010, www.royalPasseigdegraciahotel.com
Sixtyfour, Passeig de Gràcia, 64
648182597, www.sixtyfourapartments.com
Sixtytwo, Passeig de Gràcia, 62
932724180, www.sixtytwohotel.com
St Moritz, Diputació, 264, 934121500, www.hcchotels.es
Suites Avenue Luxe, Passeig de Gràcia, 83
934874159/933668800, www.derbyhotels.com
Suites Center Barcelona, Passeig de Gràcia, 128
932553010, www.hotelescenter.es

Monuments / Sculptures

Central Fountain, Passeig de Gràcia, s/n.
The Fountain with the frog, Avinguda Diagonal, s/n.

Hommage of Pompeu Fabra, Jardinets de Gràcia
The oak of Passeig de Gràcia, Passeig de Gràcia, 103
La lectura, Jardinets de Gràcia
The Obelisc or the Llapis, Passeig de Gràcia, s/n.
Monument to Francesc Macià, Plaça Catalunya
Book Monument, Passeig de Gràcia, s/n.
Solc, Jardinets de Gràcia

Banks

AndBank, Passeig de Gràcia, 85, www.andbank.es
Banco Popular, Passeig de Gràcia, 17/54
www.bancopopular.es
Banco Sabadell, Passeig de Gràcia, 120
www.bancsabadell.com
Banco Santander, Passeig de Gràcia, 5/48/82/112
www.bancosantander.es
Bankia, Passeig de Gràcia, 103, www.bankia.es
Barclays, Passeig de Gràcia, 45, publico.barclays.es
BBVA, pl. Catalunya, 6 / Passeig de Gràcia, 25/84
www.bbva.es
Kutxabank, Passeig de Gràcia, 118
portal.kutxabank.es
La Caixa, Passeig de Gràcia, 61, www.lacaixa.es
Unnim, Passeig de Gràcia, 17/54, www.unnim.cat

Entities

Friends of Passeig de Gràcia, Passeig de Gràcia, 37
www.barcelonapaseodegracia.com
Agrupació Astronòmica Aster, Aragó, 141-143
934514488, www.aster.org
Institut Ramon Llull, Avinguda diagonal, 373
934678000, www.llull.cat
The Shopping Night Barcelona, Passeig de Gràcia
www.shoppingnight.com

Cinemas / Theaters

Cinema Comèdia / Marcet Palace, Passeig de Gràcia, 13
933182396/933013099, www.comediacine.es
The Coliseum, Gran Via de les Corts Catalanes, 595
933171448
Teatre Tívoli, Casp, 8, 934122063

Pharmacies

Pharmacy Álvarez, Passeig de Gràcia, 26, 933021124
Pharmacy Massot, Passeig de Gràcia, 50, 932157019
Pharmacy Castells, Passeig de Gràcia, 90
934876145, www.farmaciacastells.com
Pharmacy Vallcorba, Passeig de Gràcia, 129
932181923, www.farmaciavallcorba.com